Putting Storyte
Heart of Early (
Practice

Putting Storytelling at the Heart of Early Childhood Practice is a brilliantly engaging and practical book that highlights the essential nature of storytelling in all walks of life and how to best cultivate this in the early years classroom. The authors use a compelling Froebelian approach to explore the role of storytelling not just in the development of literacy but also in the development of communication and language and for maintaining good mental health and well-being.

Drawing on primary and contemporary research, and presented by a range of experienced authors, this book covers the following important topics:

- The benefits of regularly practising storytelling

- Storytelling during play activities

- Group dynamics in constructing narratives

- The roles of props and fantasy concepts in storytelling

This accessible guide is ideal for all early years practitioners looking to encourage literacy, communication and well-being in a supportive and creative environment, and for policymakers looking to develop best practice in the early years classroom.

Tina Bruce CBE is Honorary Professor at the University of Roehampton, UK, a Vice President of Early Education, a Patron of CLPE, a member of the executive committee of the International Froebel Society and an established author.

Dr Lynn McNair OBE is a founder leader of the Edinburgh Froebel Network, Head of the Cowgate Under Fives Centre in Edinburgh, Senior Teaching Fellow and Pathway co-ordinator of the MSc Ed (Early Childhood Practice and Froebel) and an endorsed Froebel Tutor for the Froebel Trust.

Jane Whinnett MBE is a founder leader of the Edinburgh Froebel Network, Head of two maintained Nursery Schools in Edinburgh, Chair of the Education and Research Committee of the Froebel Trust, Tutor for the MSc Ed (Early Childhood Practice and Froebel) and an endorsed Froebel Tutor for the Froebel Trust.

Putting Storytelling at the Heart of Early Childhood Practice

A Reflective Guide for Early Years Practitioners

Edited by
Tina Bruce, Lynn McNair
and Jane Whinnett

Routledge
Taylor & Francis Group

LONDON AND NEW YORK

First edition published 2020
by Routledge
2 Park Square, Milton Park, Abingdon, Oxon, OX14 4RN

and by Routledge
52 Vanderbilt Avenue, New York, NY 10017

Routledge is an imprint of the Taylor & Francis Group, an informa business

British Library Cataloguing-in-Publication Data
A catalogue record for this book is available from the British Library

Library of Congress Cataloging-in-Publication Data
A catalog record has been requested for this book

ISBN: 978-0-367-24590-0 (hbk)
ISBN: 978-0-367-24591-7 (pbk)
ISBN: 978-0-429-28336-9 (ebk)

Typeset in Melior
by Cenveo® Publisher Services

This book is dedicated to much-loved and respected tutor Sheena Johnstone, who led the Froebel training courses and trained teachers at Moray House College (now part of the University of Edinburgh). Her legacy of committed work with children and their families continues in taking forward a Froebelian approach.

Contents

Foreword

Dr Sacha Powell is Chief Executive of the Froebel Trust, who have supported the development of the book.

It is a joy to see this unique and original book come to fruition, and I am delighted that the Froebel Trust was able to play a small part in supporting its creation. Storytelling is such an integral thread in the fabric of human existence. Many of our earliest memories will be of stories heard or told, and we reassemble those recollections as new stories. They help us to make sense of the world; our environments, roles, relationships, hopes, challenges, disappointments and sorrows. As young children are drawn into and embellish the storying landscape, we are all the richer for their contributions that narrate their own lived and imagined experiences and teach us much about our own. This book, written by and for practitioners, dives deeply into the world of early childhood literacy and educators' collaborative, reflective practice through careful observation and thoughtful dialoguing. Reading this book will help us to 'live happily ever after' (The End)!

Acknowledgements

The Editors would like to thank Manjula Devi Subramanian and the team at Cenveo for their marvellous work with us.

The flourishing of the Edinburgh Froebel Network 'Players and Storytellers' project

Jane Whinnett

Belonging to and participating in a group who work daily with children and their families

What makes this book different from other edited books on storytelling is that it is written for practitioners by practitioners. Each practitioner developed their own lines of enquiry, and the data they collected is rich in embedded meanings. Participating in their settings every day facilitated the responsive nature of the enquiries, with observation happening as and when it occurred and not on set dates and times. This participant enquiry flourishes spontaneously as it occurs and is understood in the context of the well-established relationships and shared experiences of the children and staff.

The group members are participants in the Edinburgh Froebel Network and include teachers, practitioners and lecturers from a variety of settings in the voluntary, private, independent, maintained and further and higher education sectors. One owner travelled from Aberdeenshire to take part in the group. They worked with 2-year-old children at playgroup through to children in their first year of primary school. Many of the settings embraced the diversity of the population of Edinburgh, valuing the rich cross-pollination opportunities that children from bilingual learning backgrounds contributed.

The Edinburgh Froebel Network celebrated its 11th year in 2019. The story of its origins and emergence is well documented in the *Routledge International Handbook of Froebel and Early Childhood Practice*, edited by Bruce, Elfer, Powell with Werth (2019). In that publication, Tina Bruce described the circumstances that brought together a group of heads who shared an interest in a principled approach to early childhood education and continuous professional development. Rather than the story of the Edinburgh Froebel Network beginning with a pre-set plot, the author of this chapter described it in the horticultural terms of strawberry runners. This aptly captured the way the group made connections, ventured into new fertile ground and grew new plants.

Edinburgh was a fertile seedbed for the germination of a Froebelian approach to early childhood education through shared training. There were five nursery heads who had already worked collaboratively for some time and who now articulated their practice as being based on Froebelian principles integrated with Froebelian practices. After two successful Edinburgh Froebel Network conferences, Lynn McNair and Jane Whinnett approached the University of Edinburgh to reinstate a Froebel course. Professor John Davis championed the course, and the convenor of the City of Edinburgh Council, Marilyne Maclaren, supported the link between the Edinburgh settings and the university. The inaugural course began in September 2010 with 27 students.

The re-establishment of Froebel training courses

In 2011, the first cohort completed the course Froebel in Childhood Practice at the University of Edinburgh. After 2 years' intake of the established course and well-attended annual conferences, former students expressed a desire for further continued professional development based on Froebelian approaches. They had developed strong professional relationships and were keen to develop their knowledge, understanding and practice in new areas. They gathered together as a masterclass and invited Tina Bruce to lead some opportunities for professional reflection and support practice development. Initially, the group considered separate themes at each session – observation, Froebel's movement games, schema, symbolic representation. Gradually an interest in Froebelian approaches to literacy emerged.

A Froebelian approach to literacy

Specific references to the development of literacy were scarce in accessible readings written by Froebel. He described the child who is a natural storyteller, able to draw in his peers and sustain their attention while he tells a story (Froebel in Lilley, 1967). He also describes in some detail how a child named Lina learned to write and read in *Pedagogics of the Kindergarten* (Froebel in Brehony, 2001), focusing on the role of her mother in building on her daughter's interest and motivation to write a letter to her father. However, although there are few explicit references, it is possible to extrapolate from Froebel's principles an approach based on play, holistic experiences and an innate urge to self-activity including the need to make the inner outer and the outer inner.

After several meetings, Tina Bruce introduced a chapter describing research by Nicolopoulou (2007). This research explicitly linked play and storytelling in a kindergarten in the United States. It was an approach that could be replicated through cross-pollination across different cultures. Each local setting was a cloche for the growth of its own project. The bed for the ideas was a strong belief in the value of reading stories to children and giving an introduction to the canon of literature (Bruce, 2019). Booker (2004) identifies seven main plots in stories. These themes are often found in traditional tales, such as the rags-to-riches theme in Jack and the Beanstalk, also prominent in Cinderella. Other stories include six plots dealing with the quest, voyage and return, comedy, and tragedy and rebirth.

Study groups where there is a focus followed through by busy practitioners

Interest in sharing Froebelian approaches through participation and involvement in a local group is not new in Edinburgh. In 1881, Froebel's nephew Karl lived in Moray Place and ran a small independent school. His wife hosted a visit and evening lecture given by Eleanor Heerwart in their drawing room. Gathering in a Froebelian host's home is typical of the Froebelian tradition. She was a pupil of Middendorf who worked closely with Friedrich Froebel, and she became the principal of the Stockwell Kindergarten Training College. In a letter following the lecture, Heerwart recorded, 'There is a great deal of interest in Froebel in Edinburgh'.

There is a long tradition of Froebel-trained educators coming together to deepen their understanding. Many of the Free Kindergarten staff refer to summer courses and the themes of these in their writing. Hardy (1912) from St Saviours Child Garden in Edinburgh mentions her experience in *Diary of a Free Kindergarten*. It seems likely that these summer schools sustained teachers who were working in difficult areas (and feeling they were on their own) and helped them to feel part of a like-minded community. Hardy refers explicitly to the support she received from other kindergarten teachers in Edinburgh.

Froebel himself refers to the way gatherings of this kind create a sense of unity. The German editor Hermann Poesche describes the dissemination of Froebel's ideas as 'Propagation and Extension' in the introduction of the Michaelis and Keatley Moore (1890) edition of Froebel's letters on the kindergarten.

From time to time Froebel would call together his colleagues, teachers, and friends, in 'Teachers' Meetings' to examine and further develop his system, as in 1848 at Rudolstadt, and 1851 at the Liebenstein Spa. Thither would come the kindergarten teachers to interchange their knowledge, their experience, their observation, under learned and highly placed educationalists...and to work diligently together and enthusiastically for several days together under the eye and personal direction of the master himself. Could there be a more intensely powerful means than this for the propagation of his educational system? (Poesche, 1890:179)

A sense of belonging and tackling feelings of working in isolation

As early as 1874, Froebel teachers working in isolation in different parts of the country were alarmed about conditions in school. They came together to form the Froebel Society for the Promotion of the Kindergarten System (Liebschner, 1992). Some of the early pioneering women set up charities such as the Nursery School Association

(1923), which later became the British Association for Early Childhood Education. These promoted high-quality experiences for young children as well as affordable training. Margaret McMillan was the first president, herself a Froebel-trained teacher. In 1935, the Froebel Society Summer School was held in Edinburgh.

In recent times, collegiate working has been promoted by national and local government in associated school groups, cluster working and working on the improvement agenda to close the attainment gap identified for children living in poverty. This collegiate activity time is negotiated annually with teachers in Scotland. There is also a requirement for all staff to register with the General Teaching Council Scotland (GTCS) or Scottish Social Services Council (SSSC) and to undertake a minimum number of hours of professional development to maintain that registration.

The Edinburgh Froebel Network, and in particular the group of storytellers who are authors of this book, aligns more clearly with collaborative culture, defined by Hargreaves and Dawe, rather than collegiate working:

> Collaborative cultures comprise evolutionary relationships of openness, trust, and support among teachers where they define and develop their own purposes as a community. (Hargreaves and Dawe, 1990)

Just like strawberry plants, groups of like-minded people can grow almost anywhere. However, a strong root system is essential to develop and support healthy growth. When developing any new project, establishing healthy roots is essential. The group of players and storytellers involved in this publication have studied together and through having the shared experience of the course became supported by an already established Froebelian network. Through attendance at regular meetings, it was possible to continue to share practice, learn from others and read more widely on topics. The meetings took place in the evenings, sometimes in settings but more recently in the drawing room of a large Edinburgh house that is currently a guesthouse. Each time they met, all members of the group brought food to share, and there was a social aspect to the meetings. This is a strongly Froebelian tradition.

Walter and Briggs (2012:1) provide evidence from 35 evidence-based studies of teacher professional development. They identify seven features that make the most difference. Professional development is most effective when it

1. is concrete and classroom based,
2. brings in expertise from outside the school,
3. involves teachers in the choice of areas to develop and activities to undertake,
4. enables teachers to work collaboratively with peers,
5. provides opportunities for mentoring and coaching,
6. is sustained over time and
7. is supported by effective school leadership.

All these features are present in the players' and storytellers' projects. The projects were very effective continuous professional development. They are also enjoyable, which gives participants the courage to come out of their comfort zones and to innovate.

Relationships are of central importance for children, their families and those who work with them

The majority of the group work directly with the children on a daily basis. They know them well and have had long-standing relationships with them and their families. These relationships have brought richness to the storytelling project and allowed the authors to reflect deeply on the meanings they ascribed to the observations they made. In her chapter, Lynn McNair identifies her research method as ethnographic. She highlights relationships as an essential component of the method but also recognises the unconscious bias the method can bring. Ethnography, she proposes in support of James (2002), is the most natural method to research early childhood (McNair, 2020). For others in the group, ethnography is a method that most naturally corresponds to their daily practice of observing children and recording what they see and hear. One author did not know the children as she was based in a further education college, but she overcame this potential obstacle using the character of an owl puppet as a conduit to access the children's play and thoughts and to be accepted as part of the community. Her chapter illustrates the potential challenges that conducting research in early childhood settings can encounter.

On further analysis of the group, it emerged that very often pairs were evident in the settings with one of the pair being in a senior position. This combination seemed to be productive. As well as the mutual support that this gives, each could act as a sounding block for the other, and having management commitment and support was more likely to ensure success.

Scotland has a long tradition of oral storytelling and folk tales

The skills and structure of those stories are passed from storyteller to storyteller, often through generations of the same family. Some are never written down and can develop in different ways in different parts of the country. This is so throughout the world. Different cultural contexts produce different well-loved stories which identify groups and their sense of belonging and traditions. For this storytelling group, being in the natural environment and using the affordances of nature as provocations has resulted in the stories most closely linked to the oral storytelling heritage found throughout the world of humanity.

From birth, children are surrounded by oral stories. Engel (1995) identifies the importance of the adult's role in describing the child's experience as it happens and beginning to set that in the context of the present, past or future. By telling the story of the child's life as it happens with references to the past, the adult is modelling the internal voice of the child, helping to re-present experience in language. This kind of storytelling is intensely personal and happens within a close relationship with a significant adult. The baby has an active role in it, using eye contact, gesture, movement and sound to take turns in the conversation. The story structure is innate. Recordings of interactions made by Malloch and Trevarthen (2009) and mapped visually demonstrate the introduction, development, climax and resolution of very young babies' communications.

Telling stories that are in books

It is worthy of note that almost all the case studies in the project start from the reading of a story in a book. A few have their beginnings in props, popular culture or embodied experience. Perhaps because of the industrial world inhabited by the group together with the political priorities of early childhood education in the Western world, there was always a clear link in the projects between the telling of stories and literacy.

When children are in a group setting, ways of continuing to work with and value the role parents have in children's developing language and narrative skills need further investigation. Parents can feel marginalised or deskilled. The approach used by Chris McCormick illustrates how the whole nursery community can be involved and be generators of the initiative as equal partners. This is evident, for example, when developing questions for the higher-order thinking skills ribbons which are described in the chapter.

The traditional stories read to the children have universal themes that reach across cultures, both in the values they espouse and the development of the plot. From focusing on one episode of the story, children, in their retellings, begin to link events and use some of the language of books in their own narratives. They become aware of and then use the conventions of the genre. Beginning with 'Once upon a time' and closing with 'They lived happily ever after' signals the start and end of their stories.

Alison Hawkins and Moira Whitelaw worked together, taking an approach which initially focused on providing a rich literacy environment that promoted an interest in poetry as well as storytelling. Further examination of their observations revealed to them different levels of engagement and participation depending on the group size. They questioned how effective their storytelling sessions were and considered the best seating arrangements for children so that all could be actively involved in the stories. The reflexive practice that they describe gives clear suggestions which offer guidance for others to try out. Using long narrative poems, such as the Pied Piper, gave children an insight into their poetry heritage. How much more effective is their spontaneous contextualised rhyme generation in providing an insight into their understanding of phonology than a standardised test of non-words? Every decision we make as educators reveals our philosophical standpoint.

Several of the case studies began by practitioners telling traditional tales to children. As well as having several copies and versions of the book available, the children had access to dressing up, props and small-world toys. Children enjoyed acting out the stories as they were read or told. They also engaged with playing out stories using the props.

Sharon Imray worked with a member of her team, Karen Clements, beginning with the traditional tale of Goldilocks and the Three Bears. What emerges from their work is the power of a familiar story to support individual children in times of change and transition. The story becomes the children's own vehicle to express themselves and work their way through new and challenging experiences. Cooper (2017) and Gussin Paley (1990) both believe young children use stories to fit in and to create a sense of belonging. The combination of storytelling and playing with related props allows children to retell the story and retell their own story in different ways.

Meet the authors – key themes in the chapters in this book

The research by Nicolopoulou (2007) identified the contribution of play to support children's understanding of character. In her 12 features of play, Tina Bruce (1991; 2015) highlights the importance of first-hand, real experiences that children draw on in their play. Rhian Ferguson uses an observation of a child engaged in deep sustained play in the water tray and the resulting analysis of this play as the inspiration for her case study. As well as documenting the child's scientific interest in floating and sinking, she links his play to a real experience he has shared with his family. The availability of resources that children can access or request is an essential element in the development of the child's thinking to make sense of what has happened and gain some control over the strong feelings he experienced.

Each of the practitioner-enquirers was self-motivated, having an intrinsic interest and passion for their work. This translated into an urge to find out more about the aspects that interested them the most. For Rosemary Welensky and Lucy MacFarlane, this was the outdoors. Both were trained in forest school. The focus for topics of enquiry emerged from these passions. Their case study grew from an enduring interest in one particular story that caught the children's imagination when they were out in nature. It related well to the children's own experience, had a strong repetitive structure and encouraged symbolic thinking through playing with open-ended materials outdoors. The resulting joy in language through playing with the familiar words and format in storytelling is inspiring.

In many cases, it is the power of the child's interest that compels the practitioner to find out more. Deirdre Armstrong reflects on her lack of knowledge about young children's popular culture, particularly super-heroes, as a provocation for her own learning. Her case study illustrates how finding another author's work just at the right time can support teachers in developing their thinking and approaches. Penny Holland's book (2010) *We Don't Play with Guns Here: War, Weapons and Super-hero Play* was that book for her. What is refreshing about Deirdre's writing is her questioning and being comfortable and okay with not having all the answers. By positioning herself as not knowing, she was able to find out more from the children as the experts.

Listening to the deeply meaningful stories that children tell is funda-mental to Elaine Fullerton's approach. As a play therapist and a teacher, Elaine's training gives her a unique insight into the child's world as they experience it. Helping children to tell the story that they want to tell and, in that story, being able to make sense of their experience and resolve some of their powerful feelings creates stories that are far more than a literacy exercise. These stories are a reflection of children's fun-damental being and their lives. It is so very often the quirky, atypical children who illuminate the way for our understanding of all children.

It would be easy to headline the stories of children with additional needs in the editing of this publication, but that would not reflect the ethos of inclusion that is evident in the authors' practice and writing. Flewitt (2017:8) illustrates the relevance of multimodality for under-standing early literacy, its compatibility with sociocultural theories of learning and its potential for celebrating diversity and difference in the classroom. In recognising the uniqueness of each child, we are seeing them as part of the whole, a truly Froebelian principle. The stories col-lected here show the very positive impact of diversity and difference on practitioners' understanding and the whole nursery community.

Chris McCormick and Shauna McIntosh demonstrate a similar approach to that originally developed by Vivian Gussin Paley. As well as acting out stories, the children began to tell stories to be scribed. The careful documentation of these stories and the reflection on them reveals detailed evidence of each child's progress – in vocabulary, characterisation, plot, developing a writing voice in standard English and the conventions of spelling and writing. This qualitative evidence supports the conclusions Nicolopoulou (2017) reaches using her quantitative approach employing seven measures of narrative development. The stories are distinctive, individual and show a growing awareness of audience. 'Authoring is a socially situated act of meaning making' (Cremin, 2017:5). Some children learn how to entertain and demonstrate meta-cognition in the commentary they give about writing the stories. The stories themselves are joyful.

The penultimate chapter of the book, by Catriona Gill, focuses on the development of writing in a play-based classroom for children in their first year of primary school. Catriona is their teacher and has worked with them in nursery and across the transition into primary 1. A government agenda with a focus on closing the socioeconomic attainment gap leads a drive to evidence-based practice, which in turn can lead to prescriptive approaches. Shannon (2000) describes this as 'an efficiency model of education'. This can lead to conflicted practitioners where the political agenda does not necessarily concur with the philosophy and approaches they uphold. Catriona demonstrates that it is possible to be true to your principles and use data in a way that informs practice and demonstrates the efficacy of an approach while at the same time supporting children through play.

Resources play a role in each of the approaches described in the projects. These vary dramatically from commercially produced toy characters to the very open-ended found objects in nature, like sticks. There is no right or wrong resource. Financial and ethical considerations influence practitioners' judgements about what resources they buy or provide. The simplest, most sustainable resource can be transformed in the imagination of a child. Children also make choices about what they use and often use what is to hand.

Practitioners making choices about the books that they use look at the quality of the writing and illustrations. Avoiding stereotypical images in traditional tales can be a challenge, but there are publishers who are very aware of gendered images and the lack of diversity in characters in books (CLPE, 2019). It's important that all children can see characters who resemble themselves in books (Kruse Vaai, 2018; CLPE, 2019). Dual-language books in the child's first language as well as English can be useful when text directions are the same (e.g., English/Spanish but not English/Arabic or English/Chinese, where one language text reads from left to right and the other from right to left, or up and down rather than across the page). The key is to help the child understand the language of the story. However, the cultural context of the story may still be difficult to understand. Reading these stories at home with parents can make all the family members feel part of the nursery community and allow the child to understand more at story time. However, the storytelling and story acting approach supports children very well. Flewitt and her colleagues note that:

> Even if the child's home cultures and languages vary, the symbolic play and learning spaces offered in early education can lead to a sharing of conceptual tools and systems of meaning making. (Flewitt, Cremin and Mardell, 2017:37)

Throughout this book, the authors have drawn on different approaches used by others, for example in the storytelling and story acting approach of Vivian Gussin Paley (1990) and Tricia Lee (2016) or questioning based on Bloom's taxonomy of higher-order thinking skills (1956) or story grammars (Shapiro and Hudson, 1991). It is important to emphasise that these approaches were not the starting point for the case studies. The practitioners began by observing the children and using their professional knowledge to develop approaches that made sense to the children, families and colleagues in that setting's community.

Funding

The Edinburgh Froebel Network applied for a grant from the Froebel Trust to continue to support practice development. The grant allowed settings to buy in cover to release staff from ratio to observe and write up their field notes. In this case, it was only £500 per setting. Sometimes even a small amount of funding can help settings to make change happen, and the group are most grateful to the Froebel Trust for enabling this process. Funding from another source can augment the setting's own budget and increase the commitment that the senior members of the leadership team and the whole staff feel towards the project. The resulting learning more than repays the investment and benefits for the children's experiences accrue exponentially.

The seed cast abroad...

The players and storytellers presented their work at the Edinburgh Froebel Network annual conference in 2017. There were five parallel afternoon seminars with two projects presented in each session. Feedback in the evaluation forms from delegates was very positive with several respondents wanting to hear more. The storytellers themselves were keen to hear each other's presentations. This required a substantial time commitment at 30 minutes for each project! The author of this chapter, as lead organiser of the masterclasses with Lynn McNair, devised a plan to showcase the cornucopia of projects in the most suitable venue in Edinburgh. In the heart of the Royal Mile, sharing the footprint of John Knox's house, Edinburgh has its own storytelling centre. The Scottish Storytelling Centre is a vibrant arts venue with a focus on promoting a traditional programme of live storytelling, theatre, music, exhibitions, workshops, family events and workshops. The centre describes its ethos as summed up nicely by the old Scottish proverb:

The story is told eye to eye, mind to mind and heart to heart.

It was the perfect venue to share the players' and storytellers' projects.

As well as a 100-seater auditorium, the centre has a café and interactive gathering space. The timings for the day allowed the audience to come and go, creating their own programme with time for refreshments and discussion. The day was a resounding success! Unanimously positive feedback included the call for a publication.

No one started the project thinking about writing a book or even presenting at a conference. The process of pruning and grafting to create a presentation by selecting the main themes of their work was a necessary step towards this tangible end-product. Some authors were more comfortable than others to present their work. All have grown in confidence, and some chose to present at the Froebel Trust conference organised by the chief executive Dr Sacha Powell in the venue of the University of Roehampton (March 2019). This showcased their funded projects under the title 'Messages from Research and Practice'.

Publication

This publication brings the storytelling projects together into a unified whole. There is a sense of unity and the journey each practitioner has taken in their professional development. At the time of going to press, three of the authors have just embarked on the inaugural Froebel masters course, MSc in Childhood Practice and Froebel, at the University of Edinburgh.

What lessons have we learned as educators, and what advice would we give to others who may also want to cultivate their own playing and storytelling group?

The approach cannot be transplanted to new ground by inexperienced gardeners nor grafted onto an existing plant without prior knowledge. In order for this approach to flourish, the ground has to be prepared and plants grown from seed with gardeners who know how to tend them. Adults working with children need to be trained to offer children worthwhile educational experiences, but part of this means that they also need to tune in to what it feels like to be a child, as this deepens their possibilities for learning. The final words of advice are from Froebel in a letter to his wife:

> Be in yourself both the gardener and the plant in your garden of children, your kindergarten. (Froebel, letter to Luise, 29 January 1852)

"Someone killed Goldilocks and they didn't live happily ever after…" Isabella, age 3 years

How regular storytelling helps to develop creativity and narrative role-play

Sharon Imray and Karen Clements

Background

Poppies is a small nursery registered to take up to 42 children in rural Aberdeenshire. The majority of the children attend a minimum of 3 full days at the nursery. Each day they are given the opportunity to wallow (Bruce, 1991; 2017) in their play for long periods of time indoors and outdoors, uninterrupted by adults or inflexible routines.

Nursery children can spend up to 50 hours weekly in our care. These hours provide many different opportunities for adult-child stories and chat, sharing the warmth of the engagement at nappy-changing time, song and rhyme times, or the long, rambling, fragmented story on the rocking chair.

> Children are exposed to and engage in story telling from birth and it is crucial that as the adults who care for and teach the children

that we engage in a mutually trusting relationship which will allow the child time to flourish and learn. (Trevarthen, 2002:11)

Participation in the fullest sense allows each child to feel fully connected in the day-to-day life of the nursery. Parents often remark that they feel part of the 'Poppies family', and by creating this mutual bond we can work in harmony together. Working in a respectful way with both parents and children allows a shared understanding of both home and nursery life. This helps to build deep and trusting relationships with both parent and child. One of the key Froebelian principles is relationships, and the nursery provides a place where each child is valued and feels significant within the Poppies community and beyond.

Story telling is something we all do and understand. The habit is so deeply sunk in us, historically and culturally, that we recognise our common humanity in all the tales we tell and hear, from childhood to old age, waking and dreaming. (Meek, 1996:22)

Storytelling and opportunities for pretend play are an important element of the daily routine at Poppies. Adults and children can share news, chat at together time, have a cuddle and a quiet story, tell a story under the tree with a friend – the opportunities are endless. Beautiful handmade puppets depicting characters from traditional fairy tales enhance our 'snug'. This small, quiet room with fairy lights allows for some downtime in a busy day, and children can often be found creating a story in there with a friend and some props. We value these times where children can become immersed in a story which then goes on to influence their imaginary play.

Where it began

Each term we choose one or two of the most familiar of the traditional fairy tales and share them with the children. We scaffold this with a wide range of open-ended resources, handmade by the children and staff, to enhance and encourage the retelling of the stories beyond any traditional story time.

What we have understood is that over the nursery year, as children become more confident, they begin to repeat their own versions of these stories through pretend play. Transferring the entire contents of the house corner to the book area can be a daily occurrence as they create a stage production of a story. In other instances, children have shown a preference to draw their own story and have an adult scribe for them. Furthermore, the younger child can get very absorbed in solitary small-world play, and it can be during this time, if you listen carefully, you can hear threads of a storyline.

The story of Goldilocks and the Three Bears is one of the most well-known fairy tales. We know that at home and in the nursery, it is one of the stories that children love to retell. We read it daily to the children in the first term, and as we had expected, the children began to retell and re-create it in their play.

From these initial observations, we found the starting point for our case study. We wanted to look at how the regular storytelling of a familiar tale affected children's play and learning. We were keen to examine and record the children's journey from the literal sense of the factual story to the deeply significant imaginary play which then becomes their own personal possession (Bredikyte and Hakkarainen, 2017). In other words, once they have internalised the story and it has become their friend, they can play around with it. We were keen to see if the story went beyond the nursery boundaries and into the home, so parents were asked to share with us any storytelling or imaginary play which occurred at home, particularly if it involved Goldilocks.

Thereafter, staff observed the children at play. Initially, the findings demonstrated that the children were mostly solitary in their approach. The youngest child enjoyed retelling his version of the story without the book, using characters from other well-known stories within it. One child retold through the making of a book, whilst another used puppets. Lastly, adult involvement in the play as a character in the story has also been observed.

Nicolopoulou's (2007) findings suggest that pretend play and story-telling begin as separate parallels, and our initial observations seemed to suggest this. We hoped to reach the point which Nicolopoulou identifies as the 'cross fertilization between pretend play and storytelling'.

Basically, we wanted to see how the children's narrative and storytelling would begin to weave its threads naturally into the pretend play over time.

Goldilocks and the Three Bears

The decision to continue to share the story of Goldilocks and the Three Bears daily was influenced by the work of Bettelheim (1991:58), who expressed the idea that a child needs to 'feel' a fairy tale. In order for children to be able to benefit fully from what a story can give them, they need to hear it continually and be able to immerse themselves within it. It was apparent from an early stage that the repeated storytelling of Goldilocks was going to have a positive impact on the pretend play both indoors and outdoors. We began to hear snippets of the story within the house corner:

> "Mummy bear makes baby bear's porridge... Daddy bear, you fix baby bear's chair".

Outdoors, we could see very physical versions of the story which involved running and chasing as the bear chased Goldilocks away to the far end of our garden.

Taking account of what the early observations had told us about the children's play, it was felt that additional props relevant to the story could perhaps enhance the play. Very simply, we added some bowls and spoons and three extra chairs and beds to the house area. Preparation complete, staff were ready to observe the play. Using a naturalistic approach to observation taking, we were ready to watch the spontaneous play taking place in the house corner and other areas of the nursery. We had decided to remain on the periphery of any play and watch carefully. Bruner (1976) emphasises the importance of 'scaffolding', and as a knowledgeable team of skilled practitioners, it was felt that we knew our children so well that we would know when to offer support which would then help to bring the play to a deeper level.

Interestingly, although one or two of the children used the props, the play was short-lived and had very little depth to it. After discussion our plan changed, and we introduced Goldilocks and the Three Bears figurines into the small-world play. These figurines were very popular, and within a short period of time a small group of children were playing with them on a regular basis. It was noted that the children had very good recall of the story, and the same small group of children participated in this small-world play each day. They used the characters to give voice to the story, and they generally followed the thread of the Goldilocks story paraphrased in their own words.

Seven children continued to play within this context daily over a period of weeks in a mixture of solitary and small-group play. Observations clearly demonstrated that the children had a good recall of the main characters and the events, and these were narrated in their own version with each child following on from one another as if they had a script.

Three children playing with the figurines:

Goldilocks: "I need some porridge, oh no I've burnt my tongue, I need to go to bed".
(Moving Goldilocks to the bed) "Oh no too hard".
(Daddy bear returns) "Let's watch some TV".
Goldilocks: "I'm going home, I not go to the bears house again, I sad here".
Goldilocks: "I happy again, I not sad anymore".

These small samples of play recorded through observation happened daily, and as confidence grew so did the dialogue. We were really beginning to see the play evolve; the storytelling each day appeared to be at the forefront of some of the children's play, and to our delight they appeared to be having fun with the story. The work of Lee (2016) and Gussin Paley (2005) supported our findings that the children were beginning to follow the age-old tradition of remodelling and repeating a story with a slight air of exaggeration.

Listening to the following example of dialogue, it was clear from the giggling that the ending of the story was about to be altered by one child.

Isabella's story

Isabella was one of the original group of seven children who was now showing us that she was beginning to develop her own storytelling skills. The earlier quote shows her demonstrating an extra dimension to the story by inserting some humour. Athey (1977), and also Athey in Bruce (1991:106), suggests that we begin to observe humour in children when they become able to play with ideas. Isabella had acquired the confidence now to change the story around, and she did

Figure 2.1 "Goldilocks eated the three bears...yuk...she spitted them out, they were dead and someone killed Goldilocks and they didn't live happily ever after" (Isabella, age 3).

that regularly. These new words added to the dramatic effect; she was using descriptive language such as 'dead', 'killed' and no 'happy ending'. Isabella was sharing her new skills of rearranging, changing and introducing fun into the story. Bruce (1991:106) confirms that this is showing us a good example of Isabella immersed within the highest form of free-flow play. Isabella knows the story so well now that she is taking pleasure in fooling around with the storyline. It is now 'her' story; she was changing some of the elements and exploring the age-old tradition of good and bad. She was safe in the knowledge that she had complete control of her story; if it became too scary, she could easily revert back to the safe one. Susan Isaacs (1968) suggests that in their play, children are able to escape into and out of situations because they are in control. Poppies was a good place to try this out with the familiarity of her friends.

This type of storytelling and imaginary play was not for all children, and one of Isabella's friends discretely stepped out of this scary imaginary play and headed back towards the book corner to read the 'correct' Goldilocks story. We understood from this that she was still at the literal stage of her play (Bruce, 2019), and she needed the reassurance of the familiar version.

Isabella continued to use Goldilocks as a theme with her play most days, and it flowed outdoors too. The mud kitchen had been transformed to create the stage set for the daily outdoor version of Goldilocks. The natural props within the garden provided a great backdrop for this, and Isabella generally led and directed the Goldilocks play.

The scenarios for this were short – usually one section of Goldilocks making porridge and going for a walk in the woods. The group of mixed-age children, including boys, were happy to be led and directed by Isabella, and together they took control of their own play. Outdoors the play involved much more running around and bears chasing Goldilocks. They were showing us how they could set their own rules and boundaries (Bruce, 1991) for their outdoor version of Goldilocks play.

Over this first period, children were demonstrating time and again self-initiated play using the carefully thought-out props and open-ended resources. This had provided the opportunity for children to begin to play imaginatively and more often than not led to telling or playing a variation of the story of Goldilocks. The storytelling was basic with very little depth, and there was constant repetition of the same storylines, but we were being very careful not to interrupt this flow.

Bredikyte and Hakkarainen (2017:246) citing (Heikkila et al., 2005) advocate that 'children's play often needs to be guided directly or indirectly…the how and when is left to the adults' intuition'. We decided to reflect on our own question, "When was the correct time to plan for the adult to join in the play?". We felt strongly that children needed the time and the freedom to create their own scenarios without feeling that the adult was controlling, correcting or directing the play. We wanted to give the children the opportunity to frame their thoughts and ideas through long periods of uninterrupted play. However, that aside, we were keen to see if the pretend play and storytelling could be extended to reach a deeper, more mature level. Taking account of Froebel's work, he guides us to give children 'freedom with guidance'. Having given the children the time and space to pursue their own ideas, it was now time to take the play to a new level with a little help from a sensitive adult.

Poppy's story

Wong Powell (2016:258) documents in her research of the teacher's role in play that there appear to be four stages for the adult to consider in the nursery: those of onlooker, stage manager, coplayer and play leader. Applying this model to our earlier question, it seemed that we were in the first two stages and perhaps it was time to consider elevating ourselves to coplayer.

The children were really beginning to develop the characters of the story of Goldilocks through the small-world characters, and the dialogue was beginning to lengthen and go into more detail. In addition to this, we had introduced a variety of handmade puppet characters in the story corner to give the children another opportunity to share stories together and further develop their roles within the play and storytelling.

Listening to the children, we found that they were sharing their own personal real-life experiences within the storyline, as this dialogue demonstrates.

Figure 2.2 Figurines used in the story.

A group of three girls with the Goldilocks figurines in the doll's house:

Mummy bear: "Urgh I sick I need to lay down".
Baby bear: "I'm the doctor… Why you sick?"
Goldilocks: "Let's go to bed, oh no I got chickenpox, phone the doctor".

Interestingly, at that particular time there were cases of chicken-pox in the nursery. Engel (1995:13) suggests that what children say in their stories may give some indication of their thinking and how they are processing what is happening in their daily life. She discusses that apprehension and fretful behaviours can also be dis-played within the play context as children try to make sense of what is going on around them.

This undoubtedly supported our findings as we began to observe Poppy's solitary play over a period of approximately 8 weeks. During this time the nursery was in the process of moving to new premises and the staff was preparing the children for the transition to a new environment. This involved using many different approaches for the children, including visits, scale models, plans, photographs, stories and plenty of discussion.

Poppy was also in the initial group of storytelling children. Her preferred approach to play was generally solitary or occasionally alongside a small group of her chosen friends. Goldilocks was one of her favourite stories, and normally she invited Karen, the senior early years practitioner, to join her in play. Bruce (1991:23) discusses the importance of children who need to feel ownership of their learning, and Poppy was very clear about the role adults would take within her play. She had shown us that she had a good recall of the stories, and the dialogue had shown us that each time she played with the figurines she used more or less the same narrative and order of play.

One particular day I asked if I could join her in the play.

"Yes Sharon, you can sit there and I will tell you what to do".

What followed was a lengthy period of time and play where Poppy moved in and out of the roles of the characters and I was simply to remain as the observer.

Rather than step away, I used the time to watch and listen as the play unfolded. Bredikyte and Hakkarainen (2017:248) discuss the importance of taking a lengthy period of time to observe, and by using this time to look at the outer play, we would gain a better understanding of the meaning of her play. This gave me an ideal opportunity to gain valuable insight into Poppy's logic within her play. As I listened to the narrative, I realised that Poppy was processing a situation from home the previous night.

What was most interesting was a very small section in the middle when the bear family and Goldilocks have been put to bed. The scenario had changed.

Poppy: "Baby bear is jumping on bed".
Poppy: "Daddy bear says oh no, who's that waking me up".

(All characters are taken from their beds and marched along then
   returned to bed.)
Poppy: "Sleeping again".

With the knowledge that Poppy generally followed the same storyline
most days, we were keen to discuss what had prompted the change in
narrative and what it might mean. It materialised that Poppy had just
started awakening through the night, and this was causing some concern at home. Bruce (1991:69) discusses in the 12 features of play that
children can make use of their real first-hand experiences to form the
basis of their free-flow play, in this case the storytelling with the figurines. Poppy appeared to be processing her worries through the play, in
particular using the Goldilocks character as 'Poppy'. Poppy seemed to
be dipping in and out from the real to the abstract. We could see from
the pattern and discussions that she was having some difficulties with
transitions at home and at the nursery.

The small-world characters had become an important feature in her
play each day. She would dominate this play for long periods of time
and would rarely invite anyone to join her. She would even go so far as
to hide the figurines under the rocking-chair cushion so that she could
have quick access to them when she needed them. At the height of her
sleepless nights, the dialogue became very specific:

Poppy: "Goldilocks, back to your bed it's the middle of the night".
Poppy: "You need to sleep in your own bed, try not to wake up
   again".
Poppy: "I don't want to talk to you, you are waking me up, go away I
   never want to see you again".

A similar type of storytelling was happening at home, and together we
recognised that although we as the adults could see that transitions
were obviously a concern for Poppy, she was not at a point developmentally where she could discuss this rationally with us. She was
using the small world and storytelling as a tool to help her confront her
fears and worries through the characters.

Slade (1994:82) believes that play is a valuable resource for helping
children come to terms with any emotional turmoil they may be going
through and suggests that if children can work through their feelings

and verbalise them, it can help them significantly in their day-to-day life. We were aware that Poppy had been given a new bedroom at home and the nursery was moving to new premises, which were obviously concerning her.

Furthermore, Bettelheim (1991:55) reiterates that along with the familiarity of repeated fairy tales, children can use toys or objects along-side the tale to help externalise their unconscious mind, particularly if it is chaotic and confused. We recognised that using these props allowed Poppy to create a distance away from her own mind and into the char-acter of Goldilocks. Having a preexisting knowledge of a traditional familiar fairy tale allowed her to enter into the fantasy world easily.

This enabled Poppy to connect her own confusions into the story and begin the process of dealing with her own difficulties. She was using the story to help her to work through it. Tovey (2013:24) describes this as Poppy being able to process her thoughts in an abstract way, letting go of the restraints of everyday life.

The value of repetition cannot be underestimated; it is during this time that children are formulating their own ideas. Giving children reg-ular opportunities to reflect, to replay and to act out roles from stories allows the development of narratives as well as supporting children's emotional well-being.

The role of a flexible adult was crucial at this point. Remaining as an observer rather than a coplayer in the play had allowed us to gain a very valuable insight into the reasoning behind Poppy's small-world play. We could now understand clearly the significance and importance of these symbolic figurines to Poppy.

Goldilocks and the figurines were not her choice of play once the transition to the new premises was complete. Poppy did not seek nor enter into any play involving Goldilocks for a considerable period of time. She relaxed back into the familiar routines of the nursery day and enjoyed the freedom to play spontaneously with her friends. When the time came for her transition visits to school, we found a return to soli-tary play, and she was keen to use the figurines to help her comprehend the rules and conformities of a classroom which was very different to the nursery environment.

Let me study your play and figure out how play helps you solve your problems. Play contains your questions. (Gussin Paley, 1991:18)

Poppy's play had given us an insight into how she had used her play to work through some issues and found ways to understand and manage her transitions.

Helicopter stories

Keen to carry on with the momentum we had gained with regular storytelling and imaginary play, we discussed our role and how we could take this forward and build on our success. We recognised that there were some key points to take away from this play so far. Regular storytelling of Goldilocks had been shown to make an impact on some children's narrative, and the imaginary play had provided avenues to explore emotions and feelings. The role of the sensitive adult was crucial to allow the children time to wallow in play, which ultimately gave us greater insights into that play. Both Isabella and Poppy in particular had demonstrated that over a period of time their play had moved from very basic literal play to a much more abstract mature play. Boys were not as keen to engage in the Goldilocks imaginary play indoors, and the majority of time they were not interested in the story or any aspects of it.

We knew that for some of the children the play was beginning to have a narrative structure, and we were keen to see if we could capture the interest of the boys within the story making and telling. Revisiting the work of Lee (2016) and Gussin Paley (2005), who both use storytelling and drama as a way to symbolise development and learning, we planned to reintroduce their 'helicopter stories' to the children.

Isabella was keen to get started:

"The witch came at night and she broke the fairy house…"

Isabella's storying had advanced considerably since the start of our case study, and she was creating her own stories with a combination of drawings and adult scribing. A regular character in her storyline was the naughty witch who visits the nursery at night and causes trouble and chaos wherever she goes. With this figment of her imagination, she captured the attention of some boys who were listening to her helicopter story. Two of these boys desperately wanted to share in the good-versus-evil storyline. Karen scribed their stories, which showed a combination of fantasy and truth in each storyline as they switched between conversation, fact and story. Lee (2016:23) describes this as 'reincorporation' – children are borrowing ideas from each other; the boys had borrowed the witch, added the police and finished with Goldilocks. Each element came from their experiences of nursery and home, which helped to create their own narrative structure. We had found a way to engage with the boys. It emphasised to the boys that they could be great storytellers too. Acting out their stories was equally important, and the boys took their acting very seriously.

As the confidence of both boys and girls grew, we began to see impromptu acting out of stories, mainly Goldilocks, during our music and movement sessions in the large hall. We could see the older children taking the lead and setting up their own play structures. They set their own scenes and rules independently of the adults. Bredikyte and Hakkarainen (2018:251) discuss the importance of this type of social role-play and how it can be the starting point for children self-regulating.

Having a literacy-rich environment meant that we were able to support storytelling and story writing in many different ways. Once again the role of the adult carefully observing and sensitively providing a direction for the play through the helicopter stories proved to be an effective way to continue to capture their imagination and narrative role-play.

Our final thoughts and conclusions

> A child's sense of freedom to use language in new ways to express his or her particular meaning is something that can flourish or dim depending on the environment. (Engel, 1995:206)

We established that we had provided a rich environment but felt it was of equal importance that we distinguish the significance of the role of the adult within the setting. Observing children at play is a skill. Taking time out of a busy day to actually 'listen' to what the play and children are sharing with us is challenging at times. Our case study made us realise there was a possibility that we could have missed the subtleties of what the children's play was actually telling us. Our close observations and careful listening had allowed us to support the individual child's learning and led to a deeper understanding of the child.

Isabella's development and progress throughout the storytelling and narrative was clear and straightforward. Her play showed significant aspects of her development and learning. By the end of our study, her play was at a mature level. She was creating, leading and directing many different stories within the nursery.

Understanding Poppy and what she was sharing with us through her symbolic play with the characters was fascinating. We were honest enough to admit we could have missed that small change in her play dialogue. These objects were the facilitator for Poppy to work through her transitional challenges. Recognising this enabled us to plan sensitive interventions to support Poppy through the trials of transition, particularly when she was moving on to school.

Lee (2016:27) shares from her experience that once you introduce storytelling and acting everyone wants to take part. Helicopter stories provided us with a platform for inclusion. Initially planned to elevate the play further, we found it had given the opportunity for the boys to engage in and participate in the storytelling and acting. Gussin Paley (2005:11) discusses children's inherent need to share stories with one another. Isabella's opening line of her helicopter story had sparked the imagination of the boys and their need to tell their story.

Whilst we have drawn out two case studies to discuss in more depth, it is important to remember that storytelling needs a wide variety of play. What children gain from being part of the Poppies family is a culture which says to the children, "We are interested and want to listen to your story". The daily routines, free-flow play (Bruce, 1991) and chatter over snack all contribute to the children developing a narrative voice. This highlights the importance of highly skilled practitioners who truly are interested in what children are sharing with us through their play.

Gussin Paley (2005:83) likens this to Vygotsky's image (Vygotsky, 1978) of the child standing a head taller and the practitioner alongside the storytelling child on the same journey curious to know what will come next.

Reflecting on our journey, we could see that our children's storytelling and narratives had improved. Their confidence in storytelling and acting had shown us a deeper level of their play. Significant learning had taken place for a number of our children through this work called 'play'. The privilege of them sharing with us their innermost stories was and continues to be a source of pride for us.

Tailoring traditional tales as tools for our trade

3

Transforming literacy in the early years

Chris McCormick and Shauna McIntosh

Introduction

Human beings are designed to communicate, and we are born innately equipped with the potential to develop our own narratives as we experience the world around us and to create our own stories to tell, to connect us to others. Babies beginning to babble are intent on sharing their narratives with us and, as their language skills increase and their play develops, it is the responsibility of key people in children's lives – parents and practitioners – to nurture them and their unfolding narratives. At Cameron House Nursery School, the Froebel storytelling and story playing project has built upon firm foundations in folk tale where children are steeped in stories, the impossible is imagined, stages are set and reset and creativity is captured.

Inspired by hearing Trisha Lee speak at a Children First conference many years ago about 'helicopter stories', the drama and literacy work which she was developing with young children based on the work of Vivian Gussin Paley in America, we were eager to embrace this technique in our own setting. We began by scribing verbatim children's dictated stories from play and then inviting them to act out these narratives with the help of their peers. As we developed this way of working with the children, a process we called 'Stories Uncut', we were astonished by their levels of interest, participation and enjoyment. A collection of children's illustrated stories, by then familiar to all the children, were woven together to create a narrative for a Christmas party dramatisation.

Keen to find ways of developing this work further, we were excited about the opportunity to take part in the Froebel literacy project. The initial brief was based on the theme of 'children's development of narrative skills, particularly in relation to character and plot, through play and storytelling'. The broad aims were to study and develop practice relating to pretend play and storytelling; to develop lifelong readers who will read with understanding and enjoyment; to develop this work based on the Froebelian principle of play, thus demonstrating the relevance of Froebelian approaches today; to build a learning community through the Edinburgh Froebel Network; to disseminate this work and to contribute to the local and national priority of workforce development and career-long professional learning – an exciting and timely opportunity.

Aims of our project

Building on our established literacy practice, our aspiration was to raise attainment for all children by creating a shared and multimodally inclusive context to support equity of opportunity. In working with the team to build on practice and to further staff development, our intention was to promote professional development by sourcing and reading relevant theory. Recording our journey and our findings would lead to dissemination of effective practice through training. We planned to take forward our aims through specific objectives: by introducing one story at a time, for an open-ended period of time; by reading the current story every day in small groups, working through the range of texts available and thereafter making these easily accessible to the children. To build on this, staff and parents would be on hand to read the stories to children regularly. A variety of props would be introduced to encourage imaginative role-play and the creation of new narratives to build coherence and progression. Balance would be provided through opportunities for individual, small-group and whole-class dramatisations of the stories. Our intention was to gather evidence of learning throughout the project and to provide opportunities for staff support and challenge.

Planning our approach

We chose to base our project on traditional tales for sound reasons: these stories are timeless, versions of them are commonly present within many cultures across the world and each story contains an extensive range of universal themes to be explored and an interesting and comprehensive variety of characters. Our experience tells us that children find the content absorbing and enjoy engaging repeatedly with these stories. Trisha Lee says:

> If we want our children to diversify their stories, we need to feed them a diverse narrative diet, offering them an eclectic range of fictional experiences with which to connect. (2016:23)

We started by choosing six well-known traditional tales: The Three Little Pigs, Goldilocks and the Three Bears, Jack and the Beanstalk, The Three Billy Goats Gruff, Little Red Riding Hood and The Gingerbread Man. We gathered original texts and alternative versions of these to give breadth and depth to the children's experience of literature, enabling them to soak up stories and explore endless possibilities.

Other resources

We began to collect other resources, including puppets, props, songs, story cards, jigsaws and board games relating to the stories. These were augmented with found and homemade items linked to the stories to enhance the provision (e.g., handmade felted magic beans for Jack, an outfit for Little Red Riding Hood and an axe for the woodcutter), which were made freely available to the children to use in their play and re-enactment of their narratives.

Although no formal planning took place surrounding the amount of time we would spend on each of the traditional tales for which we had gathered resources, we had imagined that children's close involvement with each of the tales may continue over the course of about 4 or 5 weeks. What we could not have anticipated, however, was how wholly immersed in each of the tales the children would become. With a plentiful supply of books, including the original story and subtle variations on it, as well as thought-provoking alternatives which turned the original on its head (e.g., *The Three Horrid Pigs and the Big Friendly Wolf*), the children's interest was high. Copies of some of these titles were added to our Borrow-a-Book Library to enable children to introduce their parents to the alternative versions of the story, adding to the momentum. As other resources were introduced (e.g., puppets, story props and puzzles), the children's engagement with the story and related resources reached new levels and exceeded any original time frame. Children began to voice their preferences for particular versions of the story and to craft their own stories. They carefully selected their favourite elements from a variety of texts, weaving them together to create their own unique retelling of the story, becoming storytellers and authors in their own right.

Story ribbons and mind maps

In response to the children's deepening knowledge of narrative and their growing understanding of the possibilities for creating and co-creating stories, staff developed the use of story ribbons as a resource for each story, to extend thought, encourage discussion and develop imagination around each of the traditional tales. Each ribbon carries a question pertaining to the current traditional tale, linked and colour-coded to each of the higher-order thinking skills in the Bloom's Taxonomy triangle (Armstrong, 2019): remembering, understanding, applying, analysing, evaluating and creating (from bottom to top).

Once children have had a myriad of opportunities to bask in books collected for the current traditional tale, 'all the same but different' (4-year-old) children are excited to take turns, over the course of a week, working with an adult in small groups of four, to choose a story ribbon. Short and long lengths of shiny satin ribbons in deep hues of purple, blue, green, yellow, orange and red are intertwined in a silky organza bag – a real sensory delight. Each ribbon is embellished with handwritten sparkly embossed words which pose a question for consideration. Each day a different child from the small story ribbon group is invited to select a ribbon. The children are involved in all the sensory opportunities this experience affords: feeling the soft, smooth ribbon; noticing and commenting on how far their arms must stretch to accommodate its length; running their fingers over the bumpy, raised letters and words and punctuation; hearing the subtle crinkle of the letters beneath their fingertips; eagerly anticipating the moment when we make sense of the jumble, the written words are spoken and meaning is made. The question is read and reread, and children ponder over the possibilities before sharing their thoughts. Their ideas are recorded on a mind map and illustrated by them.

This highly effective combination of processes nurtures the skills which develop creativity: curiosity, imagination, open-mindedness and problem solving, and enables children to go on to develop their own questioning skills. An example of this is when Jacob asked, "Why did Jack's mother not climb the beanstalk?" Jacob's interesting question, which informed staff that he was able to analyse according to Bloom's Taxonomy (Armstrong, 2019), was transferred to a story ribbon, much to Jacob's delight! Other children have been inspired by the story ribbon questions to ask their own questions (e.g., Eva asked, "What if Little Red Riding Hood's mummy asked her to go to Granny's house and she said, 'No!'?"), which in turn have been made into story ribbons. Most recent developments with story ribbons have involved sharing details with parents of the application of Bloom's Taxonomy (Armstrong, 2019) in story ribbons, which led to the development of a parents' working group. This group went on to devise questions for the story of The Gingerbread Man and subsequently to make a new set of story ribbons for the children to use. Parents commented on how their involvement in the entire process had made them feel: informed, included, valued and creative.

Most recent developments with mind maps have related to an increased focus on shared analysis of the content of the series of mind maps created by each small group of children. Some interesting observations have been made with regard to thinking skills, expressive language skills, focus, imagination, inclusion of personal experiences, reincorporation of ideas and reflection. For example, one child demonstrated the impact of his recent trip on the Borders Railway through his daily responses. As the evidence which follows shows, he gave relevant and interesting answers to each question with reference to the original story characters, and, in his illustrations, he cleverly located his answers within the context of the Borders Railway, manipulating the narrative to include his interests and experiences, thus directing his 'principle narrative force' (Cremin, Flewitt, Mardell and Swann, 2017).

The story ribbon question posed on day one was, "What would you do if you saw the wolf?"

Amos's response was, "I would run away and go on the train – on the Borders Railway train. I would say, 'Go!'" Amos's caption for his illustration was 'Borders Railway train is that!'

The story ribbon question posed on day two was, "How do we know that Grandma didn't lock her door?" Amos's response was, "Because the wolf went on the train with the key". Amos's caption for his illustration was, 'Train track going to Deutschland. This train is the Border Railway train going to Newtongrange where the mining museum is'.

The story ribbon question posed on day three was, "How did the woodcutter come to the rescue?" Amos's response was, "He saved Grandma. I don't know what he did. The wolf went on the train track then the track went back. That was the end of the wolf". Amos's caption for his illustration was, 'The end of the train'.

Within another story ribbon group, another child was observed to have been consistently answering the story ribbon question from the previous day on several occasions. These examples were a powerful reminder for us, if ever there was one, about the time children need to process information.

The reasons for using story ribbons and mind maps with the children were manifold: to offer sensory experiences of traditional tales to include all children; to encourage meaningful discussion in small groups; to extend children's oral language skills; to challenge children's thinking and develop their problem-solving skills; to feed children's imaginations; to enable children to link thoughts and ideas with words and visuals; to empower children to create alternative plots, characters and endings and ultimately to take ownership of these, either individually or collaboratively.

In reality, this way of working with the children has gone far beyond its intended purpose; the children's thoughts, ideas and information gathered on the mind maps have served as an effective analytical and evaluative tool, a means of assessment and a measure of progression; they facilitate children's own agendas, place value on every child's contribution and give all children a voice, whether spoken, scribed, written or illustrated. The value of time and space to ask, "What if…?", to share suggestions, to develop trains of thought, to revisit and extend ideas, to listen to others and to be heard cannot be underestimated.

Storytelling, story scribing and story acting

Our interest in listening to children's stories and capturing them in written form led us to seek greater knowledge and understanding of this process by exploring the fascinating work of Vivian Gussin Paley in *The Boy Who Would Be a Helicopter* (1990). As we researched the further development of Paley's work by Trisha Lee in *Princesses, Dragons and Helicopters* (2016), we were inspired to link their story-telling, story scribing and story acting strategies with our own existing practices.

Following engagement with story ribbon experiences, children are invited to have their retelling of the traditional tale scribed by an adult. Each child's story is scribed verbatim without correction from the adult scribe in order that the child has complete ownership of his or her story. Children learn naturally over a period of time to say "he ran" instead of "he runned" and "he ate" instead of "he eated" and will often self-correct in the moment if they realise they have incorrectly applied the past tense rule to an irregular verb (e.g., "He swimmed…he swam across the river".) While many educators may feel compelled to correct young children's grammar during storytelling and story scribing, this approach can interrupt children's natural narrative flow, alter the poetry of the piece and render it a collaborative effort rather than the child's own work, which should be celebrated. True progress can be documented in children's developing narratives and in their acquisition of language and understanding of grammar rules if we record their stories truthfully. Each sentence is repeated back to the child as it is scribed. This enables the child and the scribe to clarify that what has been said and what has been heard is what is being written down. The child's narrative is read back to him or her after scribing.

Following scribing, children have the opportunity to act out their own stories with the help of their peers. The storyteller can choose the role he or she would like to play during the enactment, while other character and object roles are filled by members of the audience around the edge of the stage, facilitated by the adult director. It should be noted that not all children may wish to act or have their story acted out. As Trisha Lee (2016) acknowledges, this is children's agency; children's wishes must be respected, and it should be acknowledged by all that the role of a story listener and member of the audience is a valuable one.

Deep knowledge of narrative structures and literary conventions, the affordance of extended time to wallow in the world of puppets and props, a safe space in which to wonder and imagine and the opportunity to bring narratives to life together maximise learning.

Play and creativity

We know that play and creativity are inextricably linked. It is the rich mix of play opportunities combined with real-life experiences which greatly influence children's narratives, feeding creativity. Froebel states:

> In play the child is the centre of everything and all things are related to him and to his life. (Lilley, 1967:123)

There is a unique mutualistic relationship between storytelling and story acting which enriches children's narrative development and enhances imaginative role-play.

> Play allows children to function at the highest levels of learning of which they are capable…[and]…play brings the open-mindedness, flexibility and agility of mind which is fundamental to creativity. (Bruce, 2004:157, 164)

Children learn through play and first-hand experiences; they apply their learning to generate new ideas and create new meaning, consolidating learning. 'Play is not so much about new learning as using what you have learned' (Bruce, 2004:164). The Scottish Government's Play Strategy for Scotland: Our Vision (2013:12) states that 'play encompasses children's behaviour which is freely chosen, personally directed and intrinsically motivated. It is performed for no external goal or reward'. The storytelling and story acting approach creates a perfect platform for play and creativity.

Inclusion

Studies suggest that there is currently little research available regarding the impact and value of this storytelling and story playing approach in relation to inclusion.

> Mardell and Swann identify new theoretical, empirical and practical questions that require further research and debate. These include the value of the approach for dual language learners and children with special educational needs. (Cremin, Flewitt, Mardell and Swann, 2017:9–10)

Through the medium of our project, we have clear evidence of the positive impact on all children of the processes we have developed.

English as an additional language: Some general points

Relationships are central. The development of positive relationships between parents, staff and children creates a vital foundation on which to build high-quality learning opportunities. It is important to see the child within the context of the family, their home culture and the wider community. Working closely with parents of children with English as an additional language promotes shared understanding of cultural values, practices, views and expectations. This helps to ensure the best outcomes for children.

The emotional well-being of children is paramount and must be supported in order for them to develop confidence to engage and learn within the early years setting. Children with English as an additional language will need help to establish themselves in the new setting and to build effective relationships with adults and other children. This means regular positive recognition, praise, appreciation, encouragement and feedback. The learning environment needs to be language rich and promote communication with a focus on making meaning. Early childhood methods and practice lend themselves to providing effective play-based contexts for these learners. Staff should be knowledgeable about processes of language acquisition and about best practice in supporting children using English as an additional language. Early years settings welcome opportunities for parents and children to borrow books regularly to read at home and plan for parents to be invited into the nursery to share aspects of their culture and to read stories in their home language(s).

Adults supporting children with English as an additional language need to encourage them to explore a wide range of communication activities supported by visuals, expose them to language appropriate to their stage of development and enable them to experience frequent interactions based on concrete experiences. Opportunities should be provided for them to work one-to-one with an adult, in pairs and in small groups. They need to be included in larger groups as appropriate. Children with English as an additional language need encouragement from the adults they spend time with: to listen to, enjoy and engage with a range of stories with universal themes; to create openings for them to be involved in telling, illustrating and dramatising stories; and to participate in a variety of songs, rhymes and games supported with actions and props.

Assessment methods which are descriptive, based on observation and evidence of learning, allow children to show what they know and can do.

English as an additional language case studies

Bruno

Bruno's first language was Polish, but he could also speak some English.

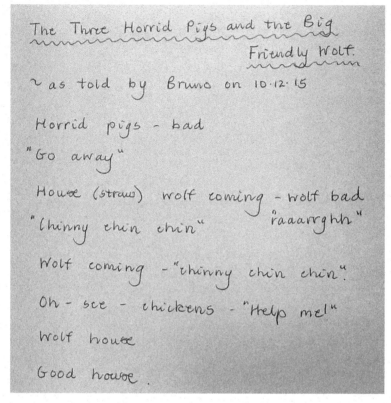

The Three Horrid Pigs and the Big
Friendly Wolf.

~ as told by Bruno on 10·12·15

Horrid pigs - bad

"Go away"

House (straw) wolf coming - wolf bad
"Chinny chin chin" raaarrghh"

Wolf coming - "chinny chin chin".

Oh - see - chickens - "Help me!"

Wolf house

Good house.

Figure 3.1 'The Three Horrid Pigs and the Big Friendly Wolf' as told by Bruno on 10 December 2015.

A series of three of his scribed stories, spanning a year, show clear evidence of progression in English language: increased vocabulary, clearer structure, fluency and detail.

Observations and analysis: half of Bruno's first story (figure 3.1) consists of direct speech. This perhaps helps him to recall, structure and sequence the story.

Again, more than half of his second story is given over to direct speech. Bruno's second story (figure 3.2) is longer than the first, has a clearer structure and makes use of repetition.

In Bruno's third story (figure 3.3), only 2 of 19 sentences employ direct speech. Bruno has developed his descriptive language to such an extent that he no longer needs to rely on direct speech. It is noteworthy that Bruno consistently uses the past tense, using it correctly in all but

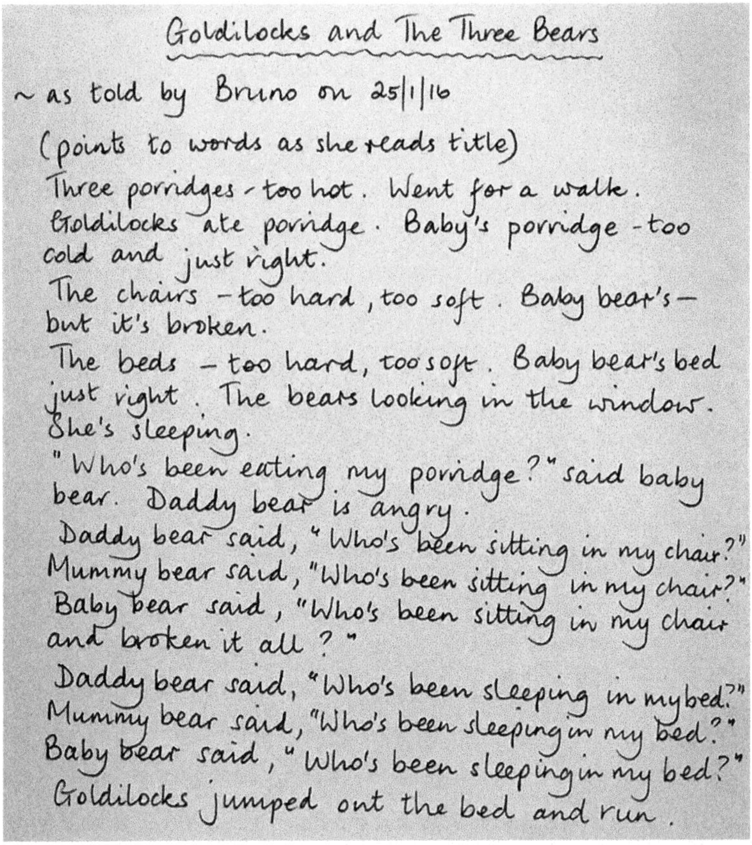

> Goldilocks and The Three Bears
>
> ~ as told by Bruno on 25/1/16
>
> (points to words as she reads title)
> Three porridges - too hot. Went for a walk.
> Goldilocks ate porridge. Baby's porridge - too
> cold and just right.
> The chairs - too hard, too soft. Baby bear's -
> but it's broken.
> The beds - too hard, too soft. Baby bear's bed
> just right. The bears looking in the window.
> She's sleeping.
> "Who's been eating my porridge?" said baby
> bear. Daddy bear is angry.
> Daddy bear said, "Who's been sitting in my chair?"
> Mummy bear said, "Who's been sitting in my chair?"
> Baby bear said, "Who's been sitting in my chair
> and broken it all?"
> Daddy bear said, "Who's been sleeping in my bed?"
> Mummy bear said, "Who's been sleeping in my bed?"
> Baby bear said, "Who's been sleeping in my bed?"
> Goldilocks jumped out the bed and run.

Figure 3.2 'Goldilocks and the Three Bears' as told by Bruno on 25 January 2016.

four instances: 'selled', 'throwed', 'hided' and 'stealed'. This is a very common error that many children make in early language development. However, this tells us that he has learned about the grammar rule of adding two letters ('ed') to change a verb to the past tense. He applies it with good reason. Children will not hear adults doing this, so it is not that children say what they hear. They say what makes sense to them. Gradually they learn when not to apply this rule. Bruno introduces characters and the scene; uses adjectives: 'old', 'magic', 'ginormous' and 'big'; describes sequence effectively; uses complex sentences with the use of conjunctions; and uses nouns, pronouns, prepositions, subjects and objects appropriately. We observed how Bruno's developing

Bruno 26.1.17

Jack and the Beanstalk

Jack and his mother stayed in a house. "Sell your cow," said the mum. He selled the cow to an old man. The man gave some magic beans. Jack took the beans. He throwed them beside the plants. There was a ginormous beanstalk in the morning. He climbed up the beanstalk and he found the castle. It was a giant's castle. He found some gold and a harp and a goose. The giant was there. "Fee, fi, fo fum! I smell a boy!" First Jack hided in the big oven and waited until the giant was asleep. He climbed up the beanstalk again. He took them and stealed them. He went down the beanstalk. Jack got an axe and chopped the beanstalk. It went CRASH! The giant lay and he was dead.

Figure 3.3 'Jack and the Beanstalk' as told by Bruno on 26 January 2017.

narratives linked with his progression in reading; by the time he left us to go to school, he was a fluent reader and was also observed reading Spanish in a dual-language book.

Franciszek

Franciszek was fluent in Polish but spoke no English when he started nursery. He heard the story of Jack and the Beanstalk along with the other children. We gave his mum a copy of the story to share with him at home and asked her to come into the nursery to translate his version of it while a member of staff scribed it for him.

His illustration (figure 3.4) accompanied his story.

In the first narrative, translated by Franciszek's mum, Franciszek mentions some characters and objects from the story. We noted that he shows an understanding of music and instruments (figure 3.5). In his description of the ending, we see his understanding differs perhaps from the intended meaning in the narrative – "he [Jack] cut this [beanstalk] because he wants the man [giant] let free".

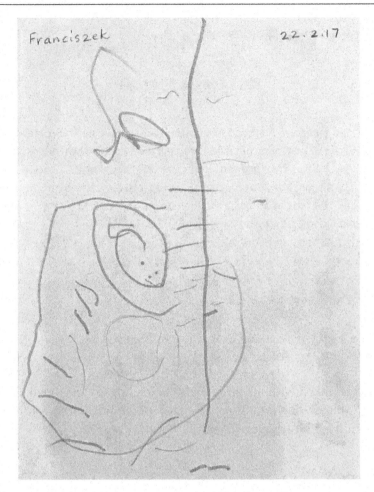

Franciszek

22.2.17

Figure 3.4 Franciszek's illustration accompanying his story.

Seven months later, using the same story cards resource, Franciszek was able to give a clear account of the story in English in his own words, which the same member of staff scribed for him (figure 3.6).

Afterwards, he spontaneously drew a picture to accompany his story (figure 3.7), as he had done previously.

In the second narrative, Franciszek names objects and characters and shows understanding of story sequence by saying, "Next one". He uses adjectives: 'big and big and big', 'little boy', 'big giant'. He seeks help from the adult and confirms his understanding then applies his new learning. He applies the past tense rule 'gotted' and uses direct speech.

Franciszek 1.2.17

Jack and the Beanstalk

(as translated from Polish by Mum)

There is a path to the home, some plants, a man, a boy and a cow. The man is giving strawberries or raspberries. The boy is climbing on this bean. And a castle, sun, clouds, flowers, mountain. Boy, gold eggs, duck, big man. It can sing (pointing to the harp). He (points to Jack) stole the duck. He's running away to the big plant. He's tied up (pointing to the giant). He cut the tree; he cut this because he wants the man let free.

Figure 3.5 'Jack and the Beanstalk' as told by Franciszek on 1 February 2017, translated from Polish by his mum.

Franciszek 22.9.17

Jack and the Beanstalk

Give beans to beanstalk and cow. Carpet. Next one – the beanstalk grow big and big and big. Go on the beanstalk and Mummy. Next one – big giant, big giant and gold eggs. This little boy need this (pointing to the harp) and bird? (puts question to adult, adult offers "goose?") yes, goose. I gotted this (pointing to eggs) and go away to the castle and music, a goose. To house. Next one – big giant bump to beanstalk. Boy bash! Mummy say, "Oh no!" Fell off beans. Egg, goose.

Figure 3.6 'Jack and the Beanstalk' as told by Franciszek on 22 September 2017.

Figure 3.7 Franciszek's illustration accompanying his story.

Both the narrative and the illustration show clear evidence of significant progression in learning.

Amos

When Amos started nursery, he spoke a few words of English, German being his home language. Amos had a keen interest in books and enjoyed sharing them with an adult or his close friend. In the first story,

Amos largely employs a story in list form. He mixes tenses but mostly uses the present, indicative of the early stages of emergent English. He employs direct speech and repetition of 'you have'. His drawing shows he is mark-making at the early stage.

'Little Red Riding Hood' (as told by Amos on 17 January 2018)

Grandma. Red Riding Hood. Bear, butter, bread, apples. The wolf eat apple. More apples. Woodcutter comes. Wolf goes in the house. Eat Grandma in here. Wolf eat. Hat. Red Riding Hood come in the house. Wolf in the bathroom.

"Eyes you have!"

"To eat you with!"

"You have!"

"Better to eat you with!"

"You have!"

"Better to eat you with!"

Woodcutter – boof! He's banged his head. The door. Grandma. The wolf's not here. Here. In the door. The wolf is in the cupboard. Eating apple (see below figure 3.8).

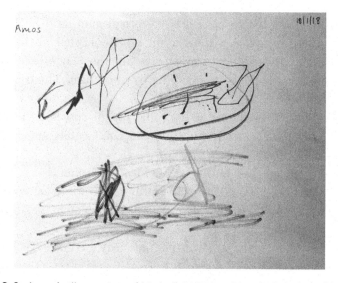

Figure 3.8 Amos's illustration of Little Red Riding Hood, drawn on 18 January 2018.

Just over a year later, in his second story, Amos is able to set the scene. Note his use of 'going to' to describe and predict what is about to happen. He is comfortable with the adult scribe, interjecting "Not me either!" in response to her aside. Amos notices the thought bubbles in the illustration and comments on their meaning, "The old lady is going to think about a gingerbread man". Note his use of the word *boil* as in a lump (on the man's head) caused by the fall. He is consistent with his repetition, which he uses to describe the action and to sequence events. His narrative has a lovely poetic lilt to it: 'on, on, he ran, until he came to a river'. He demonstrates his knowledge of mathematical language and concepts, naming fractions, 'one quarter…two quarters…three quarters… and that's the end'. His accompanying drawing is a representative figure of the Gingerbread Man 'running'. It includes buttons and features and possesses character.

'The Gingerbread Man' (as told by Amos on 1 March 2019)

The old lady is going to milk the cow. The old man is going to feed the horse – a blue horse! (looks with surprise at adult) (Adult: I've never seen a blue horse before!) Not me either! They are looking out the window. They have a picnic. And the old lady is going to think about a gingerbread man.

Here she's going to bake a gingerbread man, and he's going to fall down because of the egg on the floor. He's sitting with a boil on his head and three stars. And the Gingerbread Man is running away and they're trying to catch him. The cat is not running after!

"STOP! STOP! We want to eat you!" say the cow and the horse.

"Run, run, as fast as you can, you can't catch me, I'm the Gingerbread Man! "

"Sheep, sheep, bee, butterfly saw him". A farmer.

"STOP! STOP! STOP!" said the farmer. "I want to eat you!"

"Run, run, as fast as you can, you can't catch me, I'm the Gingerbread Man!"

The children want to eat him. They say, "STOP! STOP! We want to eat you!"

"Run, run, as fast as you can, you can't catch me, I'm the Gingerbread Man! (see below figure 3.9)"

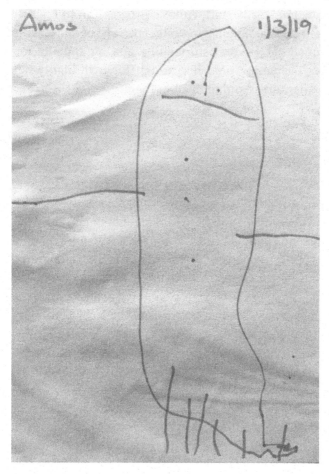

Figure 3.9 Amos's illustration of 'The Gingerbread Man', drawn on 1 March 2019.

That's the teacher; she's going to whistle. She's got a whistle in her mouth. I don't know why she's got a whistle. (Thinking and studying illustrations) She's whistling at the kids because the kids shouldn't run out the school.

On, on, he ran until he came to a river.

"Climb onto my tail. I'm going to cross you over", said the fox. "Climb onto my back". "Climb onto my head".

SNAP! – one quarter gone! SNAP! – two quarters gone! SNAP! – three quarters gone! SNAP! And that's the end!

From a slow but steady start, Amos's progression in English language has gathered pace at an amazing rate. His love of books, coupled with a finely tuned ear for oral storytelling and an appetite for language acquisition, has empowered him to tell his own highly detailed and descriptive narratives and to revel in them.

Aidan

Aidan joined the nursery setting in January 2019, aged 2 years and 3 months, with a few words of English. His first language is Spanish. Aidan's hours of attendance at nursery had recently been increased as he was settling in well, and he was then able to join in with story time towards the end of the morning at nursery. Aidan seemed to enjoy the small story group where he was made to feel welcome by his peers. Initially he was easily distracted and liked to move around the area as he watched the other children. Gradually, over the course of a few weeks, Aidan began to select books from the story corner at story time and bring them to a supporting adult to share. Aidan continues to make use of some story opportunities in this way but has also begun to listen to the story being read and interjects excitedly with Spanish words and phrases and some new English words he has learned.

Aidan's mum came into nursery to translate what Aidan knew about some of the characters from The Gingerbread Man story. Aidan looked at the book and said, 'Daddy' when his mum pointed at the picture of the Gingerbread Man. He played with the magnetic figures and said, "Moo" when holding the cow. His mum said that some animal sounds do not sound the same in Spanish as they do in English. Aidan's mum also said that Aidan had been enjoying borrowing books from the nursery library, particularly the *Pip and Posy* books. To extend his interest, we made a plan for Aidan to have a turn of taking our Pip and Posy characters home for the weekend. A few days after our conversation with Aidan's mum, Aidan brought a *Pip and Posy* book to an adult in the classroom and wanted her to read it to him. They looked at the book together. Sharing information about children's narrative experiences with parents in this way is vital to support children with English as an additional language and their families and to promote equity, inclusion and diversity.

Additional support needs

Ritisha

Ritisha had been identified with additional support needs, specifically autism, and was also learning English as an additional language with limited spoken language. Until this point Ritisha had not engaged in imaginative role-play with others. Ritisha had listened intently to daily repetition of the story of Goldilocks and the Three Bears and enjoyed being given the opportunity to re-enact the story using a wide range of small-world figures and props. These experiences had enabled her to make connections in her play. In a one-to-one situation with an adult, she retold the story in her own words using effective change in tone of voice to distinguish between the three bears. Her story was scribed, and Ritisha was invited to act out her story during group time. During the session, which was videoed, Ritisha was seen to effectively and confidently adopt the role of Goldilocks. With the help of a sensitive adult, she was able to act out the now-familiar narrative to an audience of her peers, adding in some relevant language appropriately. It was also noted that, at the beginning of the enactment, she opened the door of the three bears' house, then realised she had not knocked; so, she went out, knocked, then re-entered.

Ritisha had benefitted from inclusion at every stage during the children's engagement with Goldilocks and the Three Bears. During discussion with her parents about her high levels of participation, it became evident that Ritisha had demonstrated her new learning at home, enlisting the help of her parents to retell the story and assigning them roles in a way similar to the one in which she had seen the adult facilitator do.

Nuri

When Nuri started nursery, he was in the process of being diagnosed with autistic spectrum disorder. He received audited one-to-one support throughout his sessions. He benefitted from a deferred year in the nursery. Nuri particularly enjoyed using the beautiful props to explore the story of Little Red Riding Hood. He was especially interested in one of the wolf puppets. Using this resource, Nuri was able to extend and change the original story. Repetition of role-play evolved into a fun and exciting game with an adult.

Over several weeks, the adult read the story while Nuri listened. At the end of the story, Nuri and the adult took the puppets out of the bag. Then Nuri whispered to her, "I'll huff and I'll puff and I'll...BLOW your house in!" This turned into a game, where Nuri suddenly jumped up and waited for the adult to chase him. Use of the wolf puppet created the opportunity for him to experience the joy, exhilaration and excitement of being chased after. It also enabled him to explore drama and improvisation and to change the original story to give his own unique interpretation.

Nuri loved using the story ribbons. Each time he selected one from the organza bag, he swirled it around, dancing round the room, shouting "Wheeee!" Nuri was able to relate the story characters to familiar people from his own experiences: calling the grandma 'Mummy' and the woodcutter 'the man'. Nuri concentrated and persevered to dress Little Red Riding Hood in her cape and hood, even although this was quite a tricky task.

Nuri showed interest in, and spent time using, the storybooks and props available in the classroom for his own purposes, but he particularly benefitted from the deeper exploration and learning afforded by regular opportunities to work in a quieter environment, supported by a skilled adult. He was able to demonstrate his knowledge of the story and to explore and be playful with the content. He was inspired by the props to make links with another traditional tale he liked. He enjoyed active experiences with the ribbons and instigated development of an exciting game using the context of the story.

Grayson

Grayson is a child with specific but undiagnosed needs. When he started at nursery, measures were put in place to support his transition to the new setting. Grayson is occasionally able to join his peers at group story time but usually spends this time playing on his own, supported by an adult. He has a wide knowledge of stories and engages with story props and related resources which suit his interests and meet his needs. Grayson benefits from weekly one-to-one sessions with a visiting specialist to develop his communication and social skills.

Grayson engaged with The Gingerbread Man story and resources during the structured 'playbox' session with an adult. He looked at some pages in the book and interacted using the puppets. Grayson showed recognition of events and characters within the story by nodding in response to questions put to him. He knew that the man, the children and the animals had chased the Gingerbread Man. He said "No" when asked if the duck had chased the Gingerbread Man. When asked who else had chased the Gingerbread Man, Grayson said, "A cow!" He told the adult that the wolf had eaten the Gingerbread Man and pointed to the wolf puppet.

A few days later, Grayson was asked if he would like to draw a picture of the Gingerbread Man to go with his story. He said, "No!" A week later, towards the end of his morning, Grayson chose to draw. The adult who was working alongside him said she was going to draw a picture too. Grayson talked to the adult about his own drawing as he worked, as well as showing interest in her drawing, asking, "What's that?" The adult said it was the Gingerbread Man and the lady and the man and the dog. Grayson showed further interest and started to add detail to

Figure 3.10 Collaborative illustration of 'The Gingerbread Man', drawn by Grayson and a member of staff on 14 March 2019.

the adult's figures, such as buttons on the tummies and red pen on the faces. The adult asked, "Why have you made their faces red?" Grayson said, "Cos they been running…after the Gingerbread Man!" This was a magical moment shared (see above figure 3.10).

Grayson has had the opportunity to engage with the story of The Gingerbread Man and the story resources at his own pace, in a way which best meets his needs. The progress he has made during the 'playbox' sessions, in developing skills in turn taking, cooperation and sustained shared thinking, have had a direct and positive impact on his communication and social skills within the wider nursery environment.

Highly able learners case studies

Nicholas

The work of the storytelling project provides a stimulus for highly able learners such as Nicholas. He was a deep thinker, a child who readily and effectively used drawing and writing to articulate his ideas. He was passionate about numbers and tracking, often combining these in his ideas on paper. His illustration (figure 3.11) accompanied his detailed version of *The Three Horrid Pigs and the Big, Friendly Wolf.*

We can see that Nicholas can write his name, knows and can write his own date of birth from memory, can write the date, can use dots and dashes to represent breaks and can write numbers in order. Although his drawing contains elements relating to the text (e.g., the enclosure for the pigs' house), his own agenda is evident.

Nicholas's illustration (figure 3.12) accompanied his version of Goldilocks and the Three Bears. Again, an enclosure and the track-ing schemas can be seen in his drawing of the garden, the driveway and gate. Goldilocks, the main character, is larger than life, and the three bears are depicted in proportion on a smaller scale – evidence of his advanced mathematical understanding. Nicholas's final addition to the illustration was a picture of baby bear with 'thought bubbles' linked to the enclosure with his narrative: 'Baby bear is imagining the story of Goldilocks and the Three Bears'. Nicholas was intrinsically

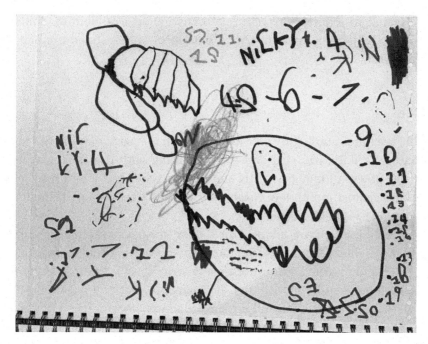

Figure 3.11 Nicholas's illustration of *The Three Horrid Pigs and the Big Friendly Wolf* on 27 November 2015.

Figure 3.12 Nicholas's illustration of Goldilocks and the Three Bears on 9 February 2016.

motivated to explore the narrative experiences available to him in order to satisfy his own curiosity, extend his interests and enhance his learning.

Alfie

Alfie is a quick and highly able learner who has a particular interest and significant skills in using and experimenting with the spoken word. He has powerful memory skills and demonstrates real joy in the seeking and acquisition of new vocabulary. He has a keen sense of humour which he uses to good effect.

When the scribe was taking Alfie's story, she paused at the end of his third last sentence and repeated the last word *oot*, waiting for clarification. The adult asked, "You want me to write that?" Alfie replied with a sympathetic smile, "Yeah, oot. It means out, but you write oot; it's O-O-T". Alfie's generous and accommodating nature radiates from his narrative.

'The Gingerbread Man' (as told by Alfie on 6 February 2019)

A man and a lady were feeding the animals and getting the milk. They were having a picnic and the lady thought of a wee man 'cos they don't have anybody. They were making dough. They cutted a shape of a man. They put it in the oven. The man slipped. He had a bump. The Gingerbread Man jumped out and ran away out the door. He ran away.

There was a swan in front of them. My gosh! They were chasing past the Gingerbread Man. They came to a cow and a horse. They ran past some sheep and they chased the Gingerbread Man. They came past a farmer.

He was like, "Stop! Stooooooooooop!"

He's came past a school. They ran past goats and the teacher whistled to say, "Stop!"

He stopped at a lake. He saw a fox. He went on it – the fox's tail. Then he went on his back, then on his nose. He got eaten with his head left oot! He got aten. The end.

Borrowed images and creativity

As practitioners we know that children bring first-hand experiences to their play and test out in play experiences yet to come, making connections. In play, children continuously build on their knowledge of the world and rebuild through repetition and modification, as Tina Bruce (2004) describes in many of her publications, including 'The 12 features of free-flow play' (adapted from Bruce, 1991).

When children borrow images they build upon each other's ideas. They employ similar themes from shared interests. Trisha Lee (2016) calls this 'reincorporation'. She says:

> When children make up stories…they see what has gone before and are unafraid of using the imagery that appeals to them, weaving these into their own narrative… In creativity we take ideas from numerous sources, shaping them to fit our needs and crafting our own individual take on what has gone before. (Lee, 2016:25)

What follows is the analysis of children's short stories which they told and shared within a small group. These show evidence of children borrowing ideas and images from one another, incorporating them into their own narratives:

> The children gathered to listen to Lyra's story. Her characters included trees, a princess, a pen that dies and falls into a well and a girl who doesn't fall in.
>
> Next it was Archie's turn. He developed his own story including a witch but borrowed Lyra's ideas of a princess, the trees and the theme of dying.
>
> Next was Summer, who continued with the use of a princess character, added her own characters then reincorporated Archie's witch.
>
> Next Riley took his turn introducing a new character and employing the trees from Lyra's and Archie's stories.
>
> Next was Silvan who introduced 'people' and a doughnut and reincorporated the idea of falling and connected Lyra's idea of the well to water.

Franciszek went next and introduced a boy with a hat but borrowed 'people', falling in the tree, falling in the water and the idea of someone else not falling.

We can see clearly from these examples how borrowing images in this way can empower children to create their own narratives. Deep knowledge of traditional tales combines with curiosity, imagination, open-mindedness and problem-solving skills and intertwines with play and 'reincorporation' to develop creativity. Trisha Lee (2016:23) identifies that 'the more experiences you have, the more things you are able to connect, the more chance creativity has to develop'.

Real and relevant routes to writing

Lee (2016) discusses the 'by-product' which comes from children observing scribed stories. She is referring to how children's

> regular observation of writing for a purpose encourages them to pick up a pen and paper and start to write. (Lee, 2016:80)

We have two perfect examples of this in figures 3.13 and 3.14.

Lilly needed support with new situations. Staff were working with her to build confidence. Lilly had declined all opportunities to dictate her stories from play, although she had often observed other children's stories being scribed. One day, when observing a group of her peers drawing illustrations to accompany their stories, she came to the drawing table saying, "I do that!" She represented the characters from Goldilocks and the Three Bears (figure 3.13). During the discussion which followed she described which character was which. The adult began to label the characters under Lilly's direction until Lilly said, "I do it!" and took the pen to carefully complete the labelling herself, demonstrating advanced pencil control and an awareness of the conventions of writing. For us this was much more than a happy 'by-product'; it was a major breakthrough.

Becky was already a very motivated reader and regularly illustrated her ideas. After enjoying several opportunities to dictate her narratives for an adult to scribe, she wrote her own story using one mark to represent

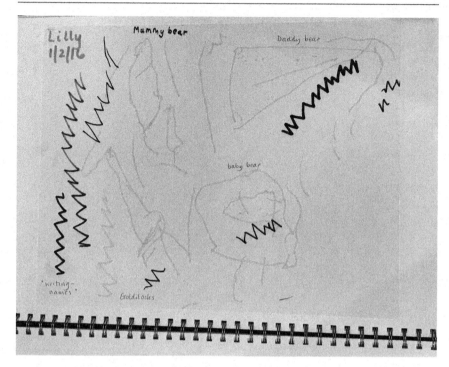

Figure 3.13 Lilly's handwritten version of Goldilocks and the Three Bears on 1 February 2016.

each word, interspersing these with drawings of the story characters. She confidently and deliberately 'read' each word as she wrote it.

However, Lee (2016) warns:

> In the UK, with its increased emphasis on baseline testing, the pressures on early years settings to develop the 'school readiness' of young children and a climate that places academic skills above confidence, independence and curiosity, I worry that a programme that engages a child in writing because they choose to could so easily become a way of getting children writing because they have to. (Lee, 2016:80)

Lee (2016) argues that learning assimilated by children, while engaged in the wide range of literacy experiences that storytelling, story scribing and story acting provide, necessitates no direct teaching. Through these self-motivating processes, children absorb a vast amount of information

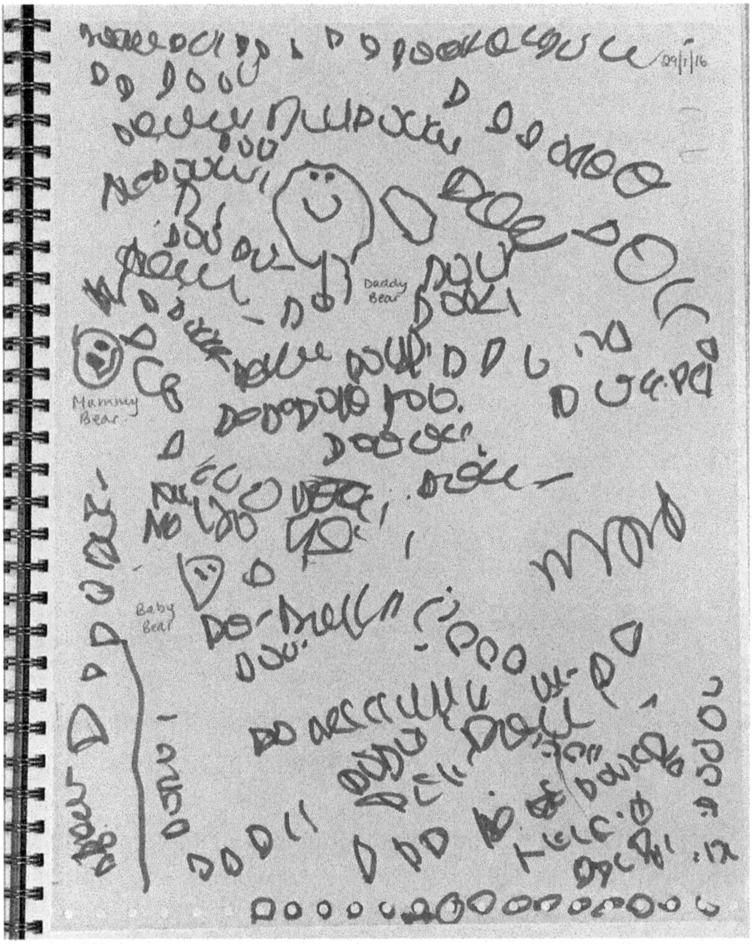

Figure 3.14 Becky's handwritten version of Goldilocks and the Three Bears on 29 January 2016.

about how the spoken word is transformed into the written word, into the narrated word and finally dramatised.

Findings and impact

The literacy project facilitates equity and inclusion of all children: 2-year-olds, looked after and accommodated children, children with English as an additional language, children with additional support needs and highly able learners. It facilitates learning in one-to-one, small-group and whole-class contexts. This approach fosters the development of the skills required to build creativity: imagination, open-mindedness and problem solving, which in turn lead to the development of higher-order thinking skills.

Staff learning, both formal training and professional dialogue around developing ideas, has taken individual learning forward and has further bonded the team. Increased knowledge and understanding have made implementation of strategies both enjoyable and effective. Observation of the impact of emerging practice has increased staff confidence in professional performance. We have furthered and deepened our own professional knowledge and understanding, making connections between existing practice, theory and policy guidance. This work provides a meaningful context for the cross-curricular learning that we know to be rich, relevant and effective.

Strategies developed within the project promote rich and meaningful engagement with parents, particularly through helping to create resources, reading stories in the nursery and use of our home library. Sharing of information and practical involvement has led to increased understanding for parents of how their children learn and the importance of reading at home.

Children are highly interested, engaged and motivated, constantly making connections. We have noticed how the content of children's narratives is consistently a combination of experience, imagination and reincorporation of other children's ideas. Children have become active agents in their own learning (e.g., they noticed that their stories had increased in length and complexity over time). The project has enabled children to access the principles of curricular design within Curriculum for Excellence: breadth, depth, balance, personalisation and choice, challenge and enjoyment, progression, coherence. Significant learning and progress took place across the entire curriculum. Children's attainment was raised in all aspects of literacy: listening, talking, reading, comprehension and emergent writing; in expressive arts: increased active involvement and performance in drama, developing imagination; and in health and well-being: increased levels of confidence and self-esteem leading to greater participation and sense of ownership. This way of working enables children to develop curiosity, inquiry, creativity and higher-order thinking skills. Children acquire the life skills of learning about learning through self-evaluation and recognising and celebrating progress.

Froebelian principles

These principles have been present in the way we have worked with the children throughout the chapter.

- learning with supportive, well-informed adults
- the uniqueness of each child
- the importance of play-based learning
- rich, first-hand, meaningful experiences
- the symbolic life: children as symbol users/connecting real and imaginary
- intrinsic motivation/self-selected tasks/children's agency
- the importance of relationships
- making connections

Conclusion

Our findings from 4 years of involvement in the Froebel storytelling project clearly demonstrate the effectiveness and impact of working in this interdisciplinary way to raise attainment for all children. As early years educators and highly trained professionals, we must be trusted to support young children's developing literacy skills in the ways we know work best, to be allowed to share in children's enthusiasm for newly found language, to embrace the joy and to celebrate the success children experience from learning in this way, rather than becoming constrained by accountability. We continue to develop, refine and embed practice within our setting and have been refreshed by the professional dialogue and development this project has fostered. We have worked to develop, and continue to deliver, training across the sector to share a key message:

> If you want your children to be intelligent, read them fairytales...
> If you want them to be more intelligent, read them more fairytales.
> (Albert Einstein as cited by Maria Popova, 2014)

Storytelling groups
Large or small?

Alison J Hawkins and Moira Whitelaw

Wester Coates Nursery School is a Froebelian kindergarten situated in Edinburgh. Here children are able to maximise their experiences, free flowing indoors and out, accessing many open-ended resources. Endorsing our identity and fostering the ethos of our community is important, and for that reason we come together midmorning for a snack and a chat and usually meet again before the children go home.

It is during these gatherings that the temptation to sing or tell a story is strong, and many times we do indeed do this. Singing together is fun, rhythmic, active and can encompass many themes and subjects which will touch on common interests for the children. It is inclusive and a wonderful shared activity. No one need be quiet or still unless they choose to be so. Listening to a story has a different effect. A talented practitioner can hold the attention of a large group in the palm of his or her hand. Children can 'hang on every word' and reach – an often collective – opinion at the end of how amazing, interesting, scary or far-fetched the narrative has been. All in all, story time can provide a comfortable, relaxing and enjoyable sojourn into the world of imagination; albeit the relaxation is frequently lost when the story comes to its end and a clamour of voices shout to be heard, each desperate to give their take on what happened. It would appear that this need to immediately verbally react is the same in adults. Recall the chattering and outbursts that accompany the curtain fall of a play or the rolling credits of a film! Indeed, if we believe in Bowlby's theory of attachment (Bowlby, 2005), it might be argued that *not* allowing children the opportunity to respond is letting children down.

'Storytelling' is often defined as the ancient and traditional way of spreading news, recording historical events, enlightening and educating, entertaining the masses or but a few, and is carried out by

tribal leaders, religious figureheads, parents, family, friends, teachers and practitioners. It can function anywhere and with merely
two bodies – one teller and one listener. It need not even require a
script – just a voice. Through the eons of history countless generations have listened to their own cultural yarns, to fables known the
world over and to personal stories perpetuated by their ancestors
and immediate families.

With the thought of examining the role of storytelling as an aid to
the development of literacy, it is necessary to delve deeper and question how children as unique individuals gain from such sessions.
Practitioners need to consider the purpose and value of storytelling in today's schools and early year settings. One reason might be,
as described above, the homely comfort of shared experience and the
enjoyment of being transported elsewhere in one's imagination. A
more cynical viewpoint might be that story time provides a satisfactory
method of crowd control (Bruce, 2019). Whichever way it is looked at,
there is no argument against the fact that storytelling to large groups is
by necessity a mainly passive experience for children.

Throughout the world education policies and curricular documents
sit alongside chapter upon chapter in guidelines and books implor-
ing practitioners to close the attainment gap between children from
privileged homes and those from more deprived areas. Across the educational board, we want our children to be excellent linguists, yet all
too often their communications are restricted to listening carefully and
having opportunities to speak only when chosen and invited to answer
a question. American professors Hart and Risley (1995) published
an article entitled 'The Early Catastrophe', based on their research,
stating that children in early childhood (7 months to 3 years of age)
from professional families, or families where at least one parent has
a degree, experience on average 2153 words an hour compared with
children from more disadvantaged backgrounds, who are exposed to
only 616 words on average per hour. This has been borne out in more
recent years by further research, and in 2014 Dr Fernald from Stanford
University (Fernald, 2014) delivered a lecture elaborating on this gap
and emphasising the importance of encouraging and supporting parents
to develop their understanding of the value in talking with and reading
to their children. Scotland, with its current aim to 'raise attainment',
advocates through its *Curriculum for Excellence* policies that literacy

(along with maths and health and well-being) should be every teacher's responsibility across the subject areas. Many writers on the subject, Gussin Paley (1991) amongst them, suggest how storytelling might well help narrow that gap.

Despite storytelling sessions being enjoyable and giving children some insight to different worlds, we continued to be uncomfortable with the lost opportunities as outlined above, to let children respond and converse. With our focus on child-led play and the importance we place on unique individuals and on relationships, large-group storytelling seemed to fall short of best practice, and when we examined its role as a conduit to extending vocabulary, to raising competence in articulation and to producing proficient readers with a thirst for reading, there seemed to be a disparity.

Acknowledging that experiential play offers deep engagement and understanding, and observing children play out familiar roles from their own backgrounds, or 'act' out well-known and loved stories, served to highlight the contrast between the *passive* role as a listener able only to respond if chosen and the *active* participation in their own play whereby the children controlled their script and posed their own questions. When afforded the opportunity, the children's manifestation of roles and actions – that which Froebel describes as making the inner outer – gave them a greater chance to express themselves and to practice communication skills. Tina Bruce (1991; 2019) in her 12 features of play, states that 'children rehearse their future in their play', and it is our opinion that this is of vital importance. Consequently, we concluded that as practitioners we owe it to the children in our care to determine how we can use storytelling in a manner which complements our approach and has the greatest benefit for all children.

We do not in any way decry traditional storytelling time, considering its place still important for many reasons, which include experiencing sheer pleasure, sustaining concentration, enjoying the intimacy of belonging and extending knowledge, for example. Nevertheless, we wondered if the age-old method of delivering to a whole class falls short *if* the aim is to develop language and literacy skills, including children's ability to write their own stories. We quickly discovered that the many benefits of reading together, discussing, listening to various versions of familiar fables and well-loved tales are more advantageous to children when participating in smaller groups.

Looking at literature on storytelling, we found articles by Greg Lewis (2003) to be very interesting. He wrote about the power of conversation and communication and the benefits of discussing and learning whilst sitting in a circular shape. The unity of no beginning and end to a circle ensures all have an equal position with no elected leader, making a situation nonthreatening. When observing our own children, we noticed how often they naturally assumed that very stance, perhaps on a mat somewhere or under a bush or around our campfire.

Although infant role-play and acting out (Gussin Paley, 2004) can extend communication skills, help develop turn-taking and foster patience, compromise and collaborative work, in our experience there is enhanced development when children take ownership of their own drama and play out either a story they have heard or one they make up, doing so in small groups. When the narrative is 'performed' in free play, we witness better learning and greater progress. Children appear to have an innate ability to create, adapt, completely alter and arrive at their own 'performance' unscathed and remaining friends with each other!

An observation noted a short interaction between two children when one threw a cone up in the air shouting, "I have a bomb", and the other child quickly steered the role-play back to her own agenda by saying, "Let's pretend that doesn't happen in the game"! Here she displayed her understanding of shifting a script to suit a changing scenario. She was also expressing the concept that you can pretend something is 'not' in the already made-up play!

How we use storytelling and harness role-play, acting out and the creation of books to support emergent literacy in all its forms – talking, listening, reading and writing

Most storytelling sessions are experienced with individual children or very small groups. A comfortable, positive attitude is laid from the child's introduction to nursery when one-to-one reading is used as an embedded strategy for settling new children. This invariably attracts others, and a storytelling session ensues. Fietchtner (2017), looking at research by Hart and Risley (2003), concludes that 'language in general and vocabulary in particular is best developed in the context of relationships, in meaningful, reciprocal interactions'. Here is endorsement of the vital role that an adult plays in extending learning. It fuelled our own belief that reading or telling a story to a small group allows children to respond. There is time for children to look at the pictures, comment, question, suggest and answer. Practitioners can recap on the storyline, reread the story and pose open-ended questions. There is no hurry, nor any distraction from greater numbers of children who might be fidgeting or clamouring for a turn to speak. It also sits well with the Froebelian principle of having well-informed and qualified professionals who are in tune with young children's learning and development. In addition, it resonates with the fun and pleasure that should be present in all these interactions.

At Wester Coates, staff share the view that storytelling not only encompasses fairy tales, imaginative stories, accounts of real-life stories, facts and information but also includes rhymes and poems – many of which tell a story. We also find that story listeners, given the opportunity, are also story writers and actors and that these creative skills go hand in hand.

We often use rhyme, traditional and contemporary, to get children acting out with finger play (Bruce and Spratt, 2011). If we take Incy Wincy Spider with its vivid description of the spider's actions, most children will respond with an attempt at wiggling fingers down the drain pipe. Reciting rhymes so readily interpreted by hand movements endorses the importance of gesture and nonverbal communication. Gesture – an extension of the pointing of 1- to 2-year-olds, and that which has led to the formality of signing – is a forerunner of spoken drama and still manifests itself widely in traditional worldwide dance, through Western ballet and theatrical works. Following Incy Wincy, it is not a difficult transition to make thereafter to Little Miss Muffet, where two children can act out the narrative. This frequently proves to be great fun, and children ask to be next to take the roles of Miss Muffet with her curds and whey and that of the spider frightening her. Several pairs can have a turn at this as it is quick to recite and offers the additional advantage of repetition. In these situations, children also experience the role of audience member. Critiquing and giving feedback offers more opportunity to use language, and expanding vocabulary, in a meaningful way.

Once a child's interest is caught, it is easy to develop the learning by interacting with the children and playing with words. Rhymes such as 'Two little blackbirds sitting on a wall' can easily be adapted to 'Two little robins sitting on a hill' or 'Two little pigeons scratching on the ground'. This technique can spark a great deal of fun and interest as other words and scenarios (often nonsensical!) are imagined. 'Two tall giants met in a lane' again offers much repetition and endless extension of ideas, allowing the practitioner to raise the literacy input and output to newer and much higher levels, that which Vygotsky (1978) would describe as enabling a child to perform above the level they could attain naturally without help, to a higher level with help (his zone of proximal development).

Children love repetition, and much can be found in books such as those written by Julia Donaldson, who often uses rhyming in her texts. Many children may know these stories from home, and some can recite them in their entirety. However, reading them as a group in the early years setting sets a level playing field from which to build. When a number of children have listened to a story together and understand its content and know its characters, the shared experience opens opportunities for discussion. When children have identified with a character, or characters, they have better comprehension and may begin to explore feelings and emotions and develop empathy. Here a practitioner can help by posing open-ended questions and perhaps (or perhaps not) gently directing the responses. He or she might suggest acting out, and when this happens regularly it becomes a norm often repeated voluntarily by children in their own play in other areas of the setting. Research has shown that when children approach their pretend play from differing backgrounds there is sometimes conflict, but when there are shared experiences the play often develops in a richer manner (Mellgreen and Gustafsson, 2011). This demonstrates a good advocacy for associating (some) stories with real-life experiences (Bruce, 1987; 2019). A baking session, for instance, could certainly add meaning to *The Story of the Gingerbread Boy*.

At Wester Coates, in addition to reciting rhymes, we read a great deal of poetry. Besides the story content of poems, we consider there is value in listening to the sounds of words and to the rhythm in the delivery of lines and stanzas. We believe that introducing children to a wide range of literature is paramount in extending their knowledge and experience. We have created many resource boxes (quickly accessible) that house appropriate small props and items to both illustrate a story and to extend imagination, should they be required.

However, we try not to be too prescriptive or definitive in these 'suggestions', and we work towards helping children to arrive at symbolic play – linked to Froebel's bringing inner thoughts and feeling to 'outer' expression. We tell and retell familiar and less familiar versions of fairy tales and fables. In truth, the word *version* is very regularly heard in our nursery! By reading, or telling, many versions we are giving the children a wider range of vocabulary, scenarios and settings. Often descriptions of characters vary; illustrations look different – due to the preferred artistic technique of illustrators – and indeed endings may differ.

What achievements and joy can be had by imagining the clothing, the speech and the reactions of the three bears as Goldilocks trespasses on their property and helps herself to the porridge! There is an abundance of learning within that one story. This can be encouraged by a practitioner's involvement. Books can be left for children to discover for themselves with perhaps the prompt of a play area looking like the bears' cottage. Finger puppets can be introduced, left lying on a shelf together with large, middle-sized and small spoons and bowls. Should Goldilocks apologise for trespassing…and if so, how? Many more endings can be imagined.

Again, the story of Little Red Riding Hood throws up many possibilities for dramatic playing out. She disobeyed her parent. Is there a consequence? If so, what should it be? Or for the child who responds to, and enjoys, more factual information, Red Riding Hood picked some flowers. Is that sensible? Is it kind? If it is deemed to be all right, which ones did she pick – can we find them in this book? Could we grow them? Equally there might follow a debate on whether a wolf should always be 'a baddy'. Think too of The Three Little Pigs! Before long a child, or children, have arrived at their own scripts with authors and writers emerging.

For those educationalists concerned with meeting curricular areas, fables and fairy tales throw up numerous holistic learning opportunities, with literacy, numeracy, expressive arts, religious and moral education all intertwining. Science can be used (Jack and the Beanstalk, for example). Expressive arts abound. Health and well-being (think confidence and self-esteem when someone reads your story!) comes to the fore, and children can use technology to print their stories.

With repeated acting out, it becomes quite easy for children to make the jump to symbolic props, usually best observed in their own play. Who has not seen a child use a leaf as a plate or a mixture of sand and mud as poison or soup for Daddy's dinner? Symbolic play can of course be modelled by adults. One successful impromptu storytelling session at Wester Coates took place while a group was gathered together due to a delay in having snack. As it was Shrove Tuesday, the story was told of *The Runaway Pancake*. This story follows the theme of *Gingerbread Boy*, which our children know well. It is ripe for adding characters and repeating lines, but due to restricted space on the particular occasion, that kind of play was a nonstarter. Telling the story from memory, the practitioner grabbed a different coloured plate as each character was mentioned. Only too well did the children interpret these symbols – yellow for the pancake, orange for the fox and blue for the river. A spin-off from this improvisation was that two youngsters were later seen adapting the technique with cups in the play house, and an, albeit disjointed, version of *The Runaway Pancake* ensued. This was (apparently) about runaway bacon escaping from 'an old man' symbolised by a scouring sponge being enthusiastically flipped over and over! Invited by a practitioner to write and illustrate their story, the children painted their depictions and a staff member scribed it. Another book was added to our library.

And talking of our library – here perhaps is the tangible evidence of how children's literacy achievements may be recorded and enjoyed. As mentioned earlier, we believe that after talking (communicating), reading and writing go hand in hand and can be developed simultaneously. That is not to say that handwriting is as quick to develop as the oral creating of a story but that once a child has gained the confidence to imagine and verbalise a story then with adult help it can be 'published'.

Nicolopoulou (2016) experimented with having a dedicated practitioner to sit at a story writing table and scribe children's stories for them. While we do not do that all the time, we do have a ratio of staff which allows scribing to be done virtually on any desired occasion. These arise when children are playing, inside or outside, and either come to ask an adult to write things down or the adult sees something of interest being played out and asks whether the child(ren) would like to have their story written. Sometimes this amounts to no more than a caption for a drawing, but sometimes it leads to an entire book of several chapters!

Returning to the thought that story listeners, given the opportunity, are also story writers and actors, we looked at extending the fun we had role-playing the rhymes, stories and poems that are so much of our fabric. However, more often than not, when an adult requested and directed, we felt we had less success in increasing vocabulary and competent spoken language. Although the various groups of children generally derived great enjoyment from acting, the retelling of the stories seemed stilted. Dorothy Heathcote (1999), who used drama to promote holistic learning in upper primary and secondary schools, maintained a child could not be forced to act. At this point we decided to look in greater depth at the roles adopted in children's spontaneous play. This was rewarding because we realised that here (and perhaps we ought to have anticipated it!) children lost their inhibitions and scripted their scenarios like pros. On occasion, stories unfolded and took their own direction. At other times children actively rehearsed (Nelson, 1984) what they were to say, returning to the beginning and repeating some lines.

Here is what happened when Freddie chose to paint immediately after watching a spider on its web. The sight of the spider had excited him greatly, and he asked to dictate his story to a staff member to accompany his painting:

> "Once there was a spider and he lived in the drain. He came out. He climbed up again".

Clearly Freddie connected his story to the Incy Wincy rhyme. Although short, the story accurately summed up the sequence of events and had a beginning, middle and end. When asked if he would like to act it for others, Freddie agreed, choosing a friend to be the spider. The scenario was short and stilted, repeating only the words used in his story accompanied by his friend, Max, climbing on a chair and jumping off while the author waved his fingers to suggest rain. However, this basic story

Figure 4.1 Freddie's spider.

evolved in their free play in our wild barked area, as Freddie stood on a crate pouring from a carton:

> *Freddie:* "Tend you're the spider. You come here and jump down and I'll pour you".
> (Max attempts to climb up but fails to reach.)
> *Freddie:* "No not like that...up here".

This encouragement involved stretching out a hand to help, resulting in the water spilling. Both boys went to refill the carton and eventually got back to their role-play where the script recommenced.

> *Freddie:* "Tend you're the spider – Spider come here. Come to my water pipe. Here".
> *Max:* "I'm spider, my name is...? What's my name?"
> *Freddie:* "Spider – you're just 'Spider'".

Max: "Okay. I'm Spider. Actually I'm Incy – I'll be Incy. Okay?"
(Freddie agreed.)
Max: "Okay. I'm Spider. I'm Incy. I'm up here. It's raining, it's pouring...wheeeeeeee".

He jumped off, but before Freddie was ready to empty said water, resulting in much frustration. They refilled the carton and started the scene again. However, with the 'rehearsal' behind them, the boys ad-libbed even more, and a story was born.

Max: "Okay. I'm Spider. I'm Incy. I'm up here. It's raining it's pouring. I like it here. I like my spout".
Freddie: "Well I'm going to get you... I'm rain now... 'Tend I'm rain" (and in a singsong voice) "here comes the rain, splashing out the sky. Rain's washing you Spider, rain's washing you".
(Freddie empties the carton. Spider jumps. Both children giggle and go away to fetch more water.)

This demonstrates how when children take ownership, learning and comprehension deepen, and they are empowered to build on their success, frequently resulting in more advanced language.

In a parallel manner, looking at how children at different stages dictate their stories, it is possible to observe developmental processes, as in this scenario. After the experience of planting seeds, which involved the process of choosing the seed, collecting gravel and adding it, plus soil, to a pot, and included looking at books and pictures depicting flower and plant parts, fruits and leaves, and which touched on rain and sunshine, three children each painted pictures.

A staff member scribed the painting of the youngest, who said,

"I putted it..." (pause) "there" (points to pot). "It's dead".

while the 3.5-year-old elaborated with a blow-by-blow account of the proceedings:

"I choosed a big seed. It will be blue – mummy likes blue, and then I choosed a green pot – mummy likes green, and then I putted soil in and then I pushed my seed in, and now it will grow".

Figure 4.2 Olivia's understanding of the natural world inspired her story.

In contrast, an older child, accustomed over the years to planting seeds and seedlings and used to helping in the nursery garden and participating in many nature walks, turned her description of her painting into a story.

> "Once upon a time there was a little seed – a very little seed – that needed water and soil to grow. So I put it in a pot and each day I watered it, until one day – do you know what happened? The little seed became a great big flower…and then it had an adventure".

Encouraged to elaborate on the adventure, she declined, saying that was the end and happily ran off to join her friends.

The stories were duly typed up and displayed. A few days later, Olivia approached a staff member and said, "I know the adventure now" and launched into chapter two!

> "The great big flower that was a little seed got picked by a mummy – but it wasn't a real mummy it was a fairy mummy and it went to live in the fairy house but it wasn't a real fairy house it was a toadstool. The end".

Much 'story writing' within our nursery comes from stories well known to the children (Meek, Warlow and Barton, 1977) and taken by them and extended, as seen in the following extract observed outside. Imagine this sound:

> "Get the rats, get the rats".

Perhaps a phrase which heralded trouble? So thought a practitioner as she observed the stampede of 3- and 4-year-olds whose blood-curdling yells were certainly distracting, if not disturbing, to those also playing in the nursery garden. After watching a third circuit of this seemingly out-of-control charge, the practitioner was on the point of intervening when that role was taken from her. A bold 4-year-old climbed onto the nearest block structure – temporarily abandoned in the excitement of the moment – and shouted,

> "'Halt…they're going now, halt I say!"

and to the amazement of the practitioner the baying crowd quietened and looked towards their 'leader'.

> "'Remember I get my money now and everything's okay".

A muttering ensued and Cee spoke up:

> "That's not right, you don't get it – the mayor brokeded his promise…remember brokeded his promise and you have to take us all away now…and we don't get seen never again".

At the time the practitioner recognised this unfolding scenario as role-play following the reading of *The Pied Piper* some weeks before. Several scenes were played out over a few days, but perhaps most interesting was the extension of that role-play a year on, which occurred when a child aged 4 (who as a 3-year-old was on the periphery of the previous year's play) brought in her version of *The Pied Piper* and spoke about 'the rat game'. It once again became a firm favourite. Second time round, however, many stories to be scripted arose, and it was fascinating to realise that some of the original players appeared to remember and took up the role-play again. When a practitioner asked a group of children if they 'knew' what it was like on the other side of the mountain the flood gates opened, and had it not been so near to the end of the summer term we would probably have had a weighty chapter book to publish!

In the same vein *The Pied Piper* stimulates imaginative scenarios of what the mountain behind the door might look like, so does *The Magic Paintbrush*. There is an excellent version retold by Julia Donaldson. When Shen paints with her brush, anything can be created and adventures follow – there is no right or wrong.

Similarly *Owl Babies* by Martin Waddell offers scope to ponder where the mother owl has been, or what the baby owls really thought when she came back…and of course there is always the potential subsequent step, "What happens next?" *Owl Babies* is a book loved by most children, many of whom never seem to tire of hearing it again and again. Several copies of this are to be found within our free-flow setting, and one reason for this is to enable staff to meet the need of any child who wishes to access this (or any book) fairly immediately. This supports developing interest without wasting time while a story is sourced. In addition, the ready availability of books allows a child to make individual choices. It presents an excellent opportunity to role-play and explore emotions…with the usual chance for children to go off at a tangent, inventing new stories.

In self-evaluating how we use storytelling at Wester Coates, attention has been paid to the children taking ownership of their learning. We have explored how we meet their differentiated points of development. Practitioners have become aware that much of the time children will happily play out stories from books, and they positively thrive on having their own stories read back to themselves and to groups of children.

Gathering together as a whole is still recognised as vital for our common identity and the fostering of the child as part of the community. However, our research has led us to acknowledge that children in their own free-flow play (Bruce, 1991; 2017) display more expansive dialogue, and we therefore try to deliver our storytelling sessions in small groups to support this.

5

Observing stories that children 'tell' in their play

Reflections

Rhian Ferguson

Froebel placed great emphasis on children's rich first-hand experiences, real experiences in real contexts which form a significant resource for play. Froebel regarded play as a central integrating element in a child's learning, 'the highest expression of human development in childhood' (Froebel, 1876:50).

This chapter focuses on several children, aged between 3 and 5 years, in a voluntary early childhood centre in Edinburgh. Underpinned by Froebelian principles, it follows the children's stories based on their own experiences and perspectives. Children explore the world through play, language and experiences (Tovey, 2013).

This chapter reflects on play and its importance to the development of characters in stories as well as considering the use of props and symbolism in storytelling. The final section considers the role of the adult in facilitating children's storytelling and suggests that supportive environments enable children to create *their* stories and tell the stories they want to tell (Gussin Paly, 2004).

> What is this play of the little ones? It is the great drama of life itself. (Froebel, cited in Liebschner, 1992:21)

Observations of Adam

A child's comment and a practitioner's observation provided the starting point of our storytelling journey. A Froebelian approach begins with skilled observation in order to understand, and thereby encourage, positive aspects of the child's development. Adam (3 years, 4 months), whilst playing in the water tray, had commented that "all heavy things sink". We had provided various objects to enable him to explore his observation. We had also just been on a trip to the local library and had been encouraging children to bring in their favourite books. Many children had brought in books about Peter Pan, and there was a considerable amount of interest in boats, crocodiles, treasure and pirates. We asked our families to support this initiative by staying for a short while in the setting to read to the children.

Parents and caregivers make a unique contribution to their child's learning. Froebel believed that the child should be at the heart of every setting and recognised the importance of the family and community in nourishing a child's development. Our setting has developed strong links with our families. It was a conversation I had with Adam's family which gave me the insight into his water play and in turn provided the material for this chapter.

Adam, the water tray and the ferry trip and dealing with fear

Adam was playing in the water tray which contained various objects – corks, tubes, funnels, small pebbles, plastic plates, cups, spoons and ladles. He was lifting up each item and placing it on top of the water, observing whether the object stayed on top or sank. Adam was deeply involved in his play and placed the items that floated to the side. He left the other items to sink and observed them at the bottom of the tray.

Adam: "The heavy ones sinked".

Adam then looks in the container containing objects used in water play. It is obvious he is looking for something; he looks at me with a frown. I ask him what he is looking for.

Adam: "Boat, can't find boat".
Me: "Would you like me to get some boats?"

Adam nods. I return with a selection of boats, large and small. Adam places these in the water and watches what happens.

Adam: "All floating. Me going on boat soon".

From discussions with his parents, I knew that the family were going to Ireland by ferry at the weekend to visit relatives and Adam had asked lots of questions about the ferry/boat. His parents had bought him a book about different types of boats. Adam had brought it in as one of his favourites and staff had read it to him on several occasions. The following week after his trip to Ireland, Adam's parents shared with staff that the return ferry crossing had been in very choppy seas. It had not been a pleasant experience. Adam had constantly feared that the ferry would sink, calling out "Boat sinked", and he had not wanted to go down to the lower deck to get back in the car for fear that the car would have sunk and they would all be in the water below.

During our 'welcome time' that morning, Adam had not wanted to talk about his trip and afterwards went to the water tray. The boats from last week were there; Adam looked in the container but could not find what he wanted.

I ask what he is looking for.

Adam: "Cars and people for the boats".

Together we select a variety of cars and people from a box. Adam piles a few cars onto one of the larger boats. He pushes the boat gently and then places three little people on the boat. He continues to push the boat, and I wonder whether the people represent him and his parents? After about a minute, Adam makes the water choppy with one hand, steering the boat with the other.

Adam: "Lots of people in the boat, brmmm. Boat heavy".

He adds more cars.

Adam: "Boat very heavy. CRASH. Boat not floated, boat sinked".

Another, older child joins in (Obasi, 3 years, 11 months). Play continues with little communication; both are experimenting with the boats, placing large and small objects in them and watching what happens.

> *Obasi:* "Too many cars, it's too heavy. It's sinking".
> *Adam:* "Lots of cars and people, it sinked".
> *Obasi:* "A fast boat, driver, brmmm, lots of drivers".
> *Obasi:* "CRASH, CRASH".

His boat also topples. The cars and people are returned to their boats.

The play continued like this for another few minutes with little narrative apart from crashing sounds. The children were content imitating the choppy movements and watching the people fall into the water. After a while, Adam left the water tray, went to the table and drew a boat. I scribed his story. His picture represented his boat with cars, both on the boat and in the water, which was choppy. Adam was in the water.

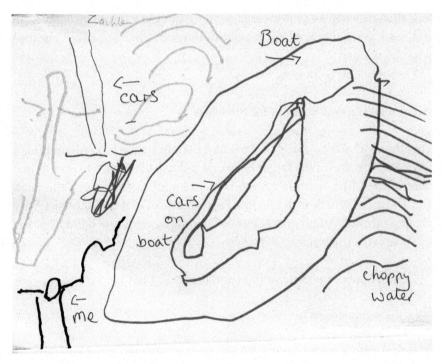

Figure 5.1 Adam's drawing of his ferry crossing.

Reflections

As practitioners working in the early childhood phase, we are privileged to witness stories which evolve and are played out before the experiences are linked to formal learning at school. The 'boat/float' example mirrored Adam's own experiences. The trip on the ferry was memorable and of significance to him. He acted this out in his play with few words, displaying the fear he had experienced. Adam later deals with this fear in social play with Obasi and Lachlan. His storytelling through his play reveals his journey.

Kalliala (2006:5) notes that narratives start as 'a small stream of events with no real beginning or end'. This accurately described my observation of Adam in the water tray. His narratives formed a starting point for a possible idea and framed the beginnings of a story. Of significance is that Adam later added different features into his story, perhaps heard from other children, yet he drew primarily on his firsthand experiences.

In the second observation, I watched the development of richer play at the water tray where real-life experiences combined with make-believe and the world of fiction was played out.

Adam engages in social play (2 days later)

The children have embraced the stories from their favourite books, and many asked for boats and pirates in the water tray. Play has developed from the initial floating and sinking exploration into tales of treasure and pirate adventures. A pirate boat with toy pirates, cannonballs and small boats was in the tuff spot (a large heavy-duty plastic octagonal-shaped tray with raised sides that contain different materials for all kinds of play). A large cardboard box had been transformed by the children into a pirate ship with cardboard rolls for telescopes, large cloths for dressing up and pebbles for treasure. An elaborate chocolate box represented the treasure chest; several maps were designed showing an 'X' for the treasure. Crocodiles of different sizes and forms appeared on some of the maps.

In their play, the children have used their imagination and combined this with their knowledge of pirate stories. By also drawing on their own experiences, their play is amplified. I observed this progression.

Lachlan (4 years) joins the play at the tuff spot. Adam has put some pirates in a small boat.

> *Lachlan:* "There's a crocodile".
> *Obasi:* "He's in danger (pointing to a pirate on the ground) 'cause he fell out in the river".
> *Lachlan:* "The crocodile will eat him".
> *Adam:* "Fire the cannonball. Boat sinked".
> *Lachlan:* "The crocodile is ticking, I can hear it".
> *Obasi:* "He's a loser" (the crocodile). "All the pirates are going on the ship with the treasure".
> *Adam:* "Too many, the ship's sinked".

Lachlan, Adam and Obasi pile all the pirates from the boat onto the top deck of the ship. Having found the treasure, they attempt to pile it on top too.

> *Adam:* "Ship's sinked, too heavy".

Then all the props on the tuff spot (fish, shells, rocks, boats) are piled onto the ship as fast as possible.

> *Me:* "Where is the ship going?"
> *Obasi:* "To the café".
> *Adam:* "It's sinked".
> *Lachlan:* "To Australia. There are crocodiles in Australia. They eat people".

Reflections

In this example there were several children interacting together. Rogoff (1993) notes that at first children's play is confined to solitary constructions, which I witnessed with Adam in the first observation. In contrast, the second observation illustrated a merging of social scripts, real-life experiences and imagination which has advanced the storytelling. Kalliala (2006:14) comments that play can be considered as 'both innate and as a culturally dependent phenomenon'. The children are active social agents, creating their own social relationships as well as producing new knowledge (James, Jenks and Prout, 1990). Obasi and Lachlan are slightly older than Adam and also bring their real-life experiences into their play. As observer to this, I speculated on Vygotskian perspectives of sociocultural factors influencing the play. Lachlan had recently returned to Edinburgh from Australia, his knowledge of crocodiles reflected in his storytelling. Obasi enjoys playing cafés in the house corner. Earlier, he had transported some of the food to the pirate ship. Whinnett (2012) mentions the benefits of having older and younger children together as the older children bring their own expertise as well as real-life experiences into the play. Having common interests and ideas brings children together. In the second observation, I witnessed the children in group play forming new connections and stories; their experiences and narratives were interwoven, illustrating a cross-fertilisation in their stories. Nicolopoulou (1996) notes that even at this early age children are able to appropriate these experiences and integrate them into their own stories. The children have intertwined their roles into their narratives:

> These conditions lead children to produce narratives that are richer, more ambitious and more illuminating than when they compose them in isolation from their everyday social contexts and in response to agendas shaped directly by adults. (Nicolopoulou, 2007:252)

One day later

The props have been transported by the children from the tuff spot to the sand tray, and water has been added to the sand 'for the sea'. A few children have gathered round the sand tray; this emboldened Lachlan, Adam and Obasi's narratives. They enjoy an audience.

> *Adam:* "Ship going, not sinking, looking for treasure". (He buries the treasure in the sand.) "Pirates…"
> *Lachlan:* "Look there's Captain Hook…and a crocodile comes".
> *Adam:* "Fire the cannonball. Boat sinked".
> *Obasi:* "He's in danger 'cause he's been hit".

At this point there are many similarities with the first story observed in the group play. Obasi places all the pirates back into the pirate ship. Some stomp on.

> *Obasi:* "That pirate stomps 'cause he wants to go to sleep". (snoring noises)
> *Adam:* "Cannonball fires".
> *Lachlan:* "Pirates coming. Another pirate is coming, he's a loser".
> *Obasi:* "Loads of pirates on board. Fire cannonball". (moves ship away)
> *Adam:* "Find the treasure". (He digs up the treasure where he had just buried it and puts in on the ship.)
> *Obasi:* "Stop the pirates, pirates walk the plank".
> *Adam:* "Fire on the boat. I save the treasure".
> *Obasi:* "The treasure's sinking".
> *Adam:* "Nobody take the treasure".
> *Lachlan:* "It's" (treasure) "gold, it's hot, too hot can't touch, it's sinking".

There is a flurry and scramble in the sand tray as Obasi puts the treasure in the water; Lachlan and Adam push the pirates into the water using a small piece of wood for a plank.

> *Adam:* "The fire engine comes". (He puts on a fireman's hat.)
> *Lachlan:* "There's a crocodile, it's got lots of legs, it's got lots of legs 'cause it lives in the zoo".
> *Adam:* "I been to a zoo, the crocodile has a trunk".
> *Obasi:* "Get the treasure".
> *Lachlan:* "There's a hill with the crocodile and there's Captain Hook. Captain Hook's scared of the crocodile".
> *Obasi:* "I'm not scared of the crocodile". (He scrambles in the sand for the treasure.)
> *Lachlan:* "We can hear the crocodile coming, he ate the clock, it's ticking. The crocodile will scare the people then we can get the treasure".
> *Obasi:* "Treasure, we need treasure". (Lots of sand falling out of the tray. The children place all the treasure they have found in a small bucket.)

At this point Cora (5 years), who has been dressing up in beads, a blanket, headscarf and tiara, comes up slowly to the sand tray. She has been playing on her own for a while but listening to the conversations. She picks up two stones which have fallen out of the sand tray, looks at them and then at the boys.

> *Obasi:* "Are you a pirate?"
>
> *Cora:* "No, I am a 'pirate princess'. I am looking for treasure". (There is a long pause as the others take in her words and appearance. She continues.)
>
> *Cora:* "I am the 'pirate princess'. I wear princess clothes. I live in a boat with my brother and family and we watch dolphins. Me and my brother speak to the dolphins, I have dolphins in my bed, they telled me about treasure and their babies. I have lots of treasure, I need more for the dolphins. (She hands over a basket.)

At this point there is silence and the children at the sand tray place the stones from the tray into her basket. Cora takes the basket to the dressing-up area, removes her props and goes to have snack, the interest in her role seemingly vanished.

Play continues but the children appear subdued without the treasure. However, Obasi then takes on a new thread for the story…

> *Obasi:* "Did you see the crocodile?"
> *Lachlan:* "Let's find the ticking…"

Reflections

Real-life experiences, interwoven with fictional stories of 'treasure and crocodiles', have motivated the stories in the third observation. Lachlan and Cora have introduced their own experiences which enhanced and developed the narratives. As an observer I witnessed their play as an expression of their understanding of the world around them (Bruce, 2012). Often younger children's narratives are repetitive, and first attempts to reproduce stories can be disjointed. The third case study has a mixture of the children genuinely applying their knowledge from the books and their own experiences to their narratives. Cora's arrival

Figure 5.2 The pirate princess.

as the pirate princess heightened the children's interest and emotional engagement in their play (Nicolopoulou, 2007).

Play

> The challenge…when we think about play is that it can be misinter-preted as being 'just play' and the intrinsic value of what a child is actually doing can be missed or ignored and therefore seen as less valued. It is both a tricky word and complicated concept to define. (Building the Ambition, 2014:28)

Play is not trivial; it is highly serious and of deep significance (Froebel, 1826), and it is central to a Froebelian approach. This was reflected by Adam's play in the water tray where he tried to come to terms with his feelings from his ferry trip. The early pioneers emphasised the importance of play as crucial to children's emotional health. Play therefore feeds on first-hand experiences; yet Bruce (1991) notes that providing play materials on their own is not sufficient. Adam had used play, mark-making and a small amount of narration to try and understand his feelings and experiences. In the setting I watched, Adam playing out something in his mind which he had experienced in his past. Froebel wrote about making the inner outer. Adam used his play to coordinate his experiences and ideas to connect his thoughts with his inner feelings. It is a learning process for him. Play can therefore be an integrating mechanism and a powerful matrix for learning as well (Bruce, 2015).

The re-enactment of the boat trip amplifies the importance of first-hand experiences which are then enriched and expanded through play. Susan Isaacs notes that deep, rich play enables children to be more themselves; the child 'reveal(s) himself in his play' (Dunlop, 2018:218, quoting Isaacs, 1954:6). We have observed this with Adam revealing his feelings in his play.

Nor is play static (Tovey, 2013). We have followed the children's storytelling which has journeyed from the water tray, to easel, to tuff spot and sand tray. We have observed that rich play needs space; what started in one area has overflowed to other areas.

The observations further demonstrate the importance of play to help children understand their emotions. Play builds connections between the outer world of new experiences (Adam and the ferry trip) and the inner world of ideas and imaginations. This cross-fertilisation is revealed in the reworking of themes from the children's own stories and experiences. They introduced the crocodile which swallowed the clock from their knowledge of *Peter Pan*. However, their stories also demonstrated a considerable incoherence and a lack of sustained thematic interchange. Nevertheless, the observations have illustrated the children learning with and through each other in their cooperative play. Kavanaugh and Engel (1998) note that this is a very valuable development as it lays down critical foundations for discursive narrative skills such as thematic unity at a later stage. As observers we have witnessed the reworking of familiar themes of stories in parallel play – for example, the ticking crocodile and searching for treasure. However, we have also perceived play guiding the process of story-telling, giving the children a sense of agency. The story they tell is theirs; they have created, developed and delivered it.

Symbolic representations

> In make-believe play the players not only experience something of a fantasy world but also change into imagined persons and act accordingly. (Kalliala, 2006:21)

As an observer I watched Adam immersed in his play. He used the boats, cars and small-world people to re-enact his boat trip. The props supported his activities, drawing him into a world of real and imagined experiences. Winnicott (1971) described this area as one of free activity which lies between a world of verifiable experiences and an inner world which draws on knowledge and life experiences. The props enable Adam to re-enact his experience of his trip on the ferry.

Children also need a wide range of experiences to draw on and opportunities to represent their inner meanings in outward representations. Adam's picture is an extended part of his story; his inner contemplations are revealed in his outer representations. He chose drawing as the medium to expand his story. Tovey (2013) suggests that writing is a complex form of symbolic representation; wearing the fireman's helmet helped Adam enter into his imaginary world and extend his story. Similarly, Cora used dressing-up props to tell her story. The props supported her to enter the safe imagined world of the pirate princess. She was in control and made up her own rules. The props liberated her to go beyond the here and now (Bruner, 1986), taking her beyond a literal world which can often be restricted by the constructs and formalities of language. Such structures can inhibit the expression of these imaginations and hinder the storytelling. Cora has used clothes as her props and her knowledge of princesses to tell her story.

The use of symbolic representation thus extended the children's narratives and removed the limitations of verbal language. Cora drew on her interpretation of princesses to enter her fantasy world. She seemed detached from reality. In the children's narrations, we witnessed spontaneous inventions and sudden changes without a predictable and inevitable ending. Kalliala (2006) notes that as part of fantasy play children play out their needs. Cora needed to perform her story and hold the stage. She was freed of any structural constraints (Burgess, 1988). The dressing-up props have defined her story. She is 'trying on stories, like clothes' (Stanzel, 1984:109, quoting Frisch, 1964). After she obtained the treasure, she discarded her clothes and identity and went to have snack. Her story was complete. Drawing on her imagination, creativity and experiences has enabled her to move from real to fantasy worlds with ease (Kalliala, 2006). Adults find this more difficult.

To conclude this section, it was noticeable that the children used the props to enhance their storytelling. They have also applied their own experiences, their knowledge from books and their relationships with others to support their storytelling. A sensitive adult who can facilitate children's play and extend their narratives is the focus of the next section.

Role of the adult

A Froebelian approach places emphasis on rich first hand experience, a challenging environment but also informed, sensitive adults. (Tovey, 2013:29)

Triggered by a child's observation that 'all heavy things sink', we had been examining objects which floated and sank. Adam's play in the water tray after his ferry crossing was quite different to his play prior to the trip. On his return his play reflected his experiences on the ferry. Adam had been experimenting with the concept that all things heavy sink; part of his fear was that a boat is heavy, and heavy things sink. He had never been on a boat before, but the crossing had given him direct experience that all heavy things do not sink. On returning to the water tray he explored not only his feelings but also the new knowledge that his experiences had given him. He wanted some toys to play out this experience. I provided them and was able to help Adam 'build bridges between experiences and learning' (Gussin Paley, 2004:8).

The adult's role is multifarious and crucial. My role was that of facilitator, someone who steps back and watches, who does not push on with an agenda for children's learning. In this situation, I gave Adam time and space to tell his story. Nicolopoulou, McDowell and Brockmeyer (2006) note that this can be most effective when play is successfully combined with both child-centred and practitioner-led approaches. Froebel calls this 'freedom with guidance' (Bruce, 2019; Tovey, 2017).

As adults we need to provide an enabling early years environment which allows children to choose, take control, explore, imagine and lose themselves in their creativity. Remaining in control of their play is paramount:

> The adult who if too passive or prescriptive in child centred education will result in annihilating, hindering and destroying the play. (Entwhistle, 1970:142)

An experienced and educated workforce with knowledge of child development is required. An adult who takes on a more active directing role is potentially disruptive to early development. It is pointless to push on with an adult agenda for children's learning when there are no links to children's current understanding (Tovey, 2013). Nicolopoulou (2007) underlines the important contribution of real-life experiences to storytelling as well as a sensitive adult:

> [Children use] discursive narratives to make sense of their experiences supported by adult-child talk. (Nicolopoulou, 2007:250)

Supportive adults help children merge their play and narratives. These can often appear as separate activities. Adam's water-tray activities involved playing with the boats and people whilst uttering little proto-narratives. The role I played was supportive. As an adult I gave him the props he wanted to experiment with. This extended his thinking. The Scottish government document *Building the Ambition* (2014) highlights Froebelian principles regarding the adult role, suggesting that

> the practitioner is of critical importance if young children are going to extend their thinking, widen their learning and consolidate their learning in play. (Building the Ambition, 2014:29)

As practitioners we may be tempted to bring in many learning activities – or what we perceive as learning activities but which have no meaning to the child. Supporting children's narrative activity cannot

be achieved through training children in technical skills such as letter and word recognition alone. During our masterclass sessions, we
discussed the importance of meaningful activities for children and the
dangers of trying to over-plan the early childhood curriculum, which
would cut across play in a deeply damaging way (Edinburgh Froebel
masterclass, April 2016). A Froebelian pedagogy would encourage the
learner to take the initiative. This enables the learner to engage in deep
learning rather than surface learning. The most effective approach to
the development of reading and writing is to provide children with
what they need. Vygotsky (1976) notes that children, when playing, are
operating at their highest level possible, the 'zone of proximal development', which corresponds with their future developmental level, a
level they are able to reach with the help of an adult. As adults, we need
to provide guidance and freedom for the child in a sensitive, nondirec-
tive way. Adam's play had meaning, he had control of his play and
he chose the pace of his play. This supports Tovey's (2013) view that
children need supportive, skilled practitioners who provide freedom
with guidance.

Conclusion

'In constructing their stories, the children drew themes, characters,
images, plots and other elements from each other's stories. They also
incorporated elements into their narratives from a wide range of other
sources, including fairy tales, children's books…and their own experience' (Nicolopoulou, 2007:253).

This quote from Nicolopoulou, who informed my research, endorses
my findings in this chapter. Froebelian principles provide a framework which underpins the observations and reflections. Adam's play
in the water tray formed a starting point for a possible idea or make-
believe tale, shaping the beginnings of an imaginary world. His initial
explorations have developed from solitary proto-narratives into active
participation and re-enactment of his story with others. The symbolic
representations and props have supported the children's use of creativity and fantasy as a tool to grapple with reality and master the
larger social worlds they live in. The children have ownership of their
stories.

The adult role is crucial in facilitating both play and a child's story. Sensitive adults help support the children to develop knowledge themselves rather than deposit their own ideas on the child (Aliakbar and Faraji, 2011). Viewing the child as a learner in his own right rejects a banking model of education (Freire, 1993) and empowers children to see themselves as competent learners.

In conclusion, mastering narrative skills in the early childhood years is a crucial foundation for emergent literature and storytelling. It supports successful development at school (Nicolopoulou, 2007). Encouraging children's narrative activity and oral language skills is an essential foundation of emergent literacy. Stories are inherent in a child's being; they are not secondary mental constructs. As practitioners, it is our role to support children and provide rich play experiences to enable them to tell the stories they want to tell.

The key findings in this chapter are that a Froebelian approach gives children experiences instead of instruction. The focus is on activities, not outcomes. Rich and meaningful first-hand experiences are central to play and learning. Play helps children organise and bring together learning. It helps develop symbolic thought and abstract thinking. Language is not only verbal but also nonverbal. Children communicate in many different ways; language can be symbolically represented. Everyone working with young children recognises the importance of the child's family and community to understand the child and his or her development. Older children bring an expertise to the experiences of younger children. Froebel recognised how children learn with and through each other. The difference between what play is and what it is not is the control the child has over the activity. Children and adults play and learn together. Skilled practitioners are those who are well educated, well trained and informed about the development of children, as well as observers who can tune in to the child's needs and requirements.

Using props

An adventure in stories and drama to encourage young storytellers

Lynda Bardai

Introduction

This chapter traces the story of the longevity of a prop. It shows the journey taken and the positive effect of a story bag, which through the years has encouraged and, on occasion, ignited the imagination of children to develop their own stories. These have been spoken, dramatised and at times written down.

> Every human being has stories to be told, if there is somebody who has the interest to listen to them. (Riihelda in Anderson, 2008:23)

This resonated with me. As professionals and fellow citizens, we need to listen carefully to the stories of others. By doing so we enable connectivity with all who share our world, whether through work or play. Those working directly with young children strive to connect sensitively with the inner thoughts of the child (Froebel, 1898). The story bag can be a very effective tool.

An idea is realised

When I was a Nursery Nurse Examination Board student, I was required to complete a project to develop a prop to assist children's imagination and connection with the spoken and written word – a prop that could be used to advance children's engagement with stories. I decided to make a story bag to hold different items for stories that the children or I could choose to illustrate. These stories could be either the development of well-known tales or the children's own stories. At the time I never gave any thought to the fact that 40 years later I would still be using this story bag.

Early childhood provision then was very different to that of today. In the 1970s nursery provision in Scotland was divided into day nursery provided by Social Work and Nursery Schools and classes provided by Education. There was little private provision other than nannies working closely with families. At that time there was a much less defined curriculum. It is therefore important to understand the historical context of how the bag was used. Moss (2014:37) critiques the 'schoolification' of nursery and advocates that early childhood settings should incorporate 'a story of democracy, experimentation and potentiality' (2014:139) which is more congruent with early childhood learning and can be achieved through children's involvement in researching their own stories. It is in experimenting with this approach that I have found my story bag to be valuable. It is important for the story bag to have meaning in the child's learning. Children need to feel ownership.

This contrasts with the main focus of creating stories using the story bag in the early days when enjoyment was the central aim. However, enjoyment is not enough. If children are passive receivers of stories, there is little story development or active connection with the narratives of the stories. There was some acting out of well-known stories and play with props, but there was no real story development. Perhaps the story bag resonates with Froebel's use of his coat with deep pockets as a tool to hold treasures for the children to explore. I realise now that his teaching was not so much to do with the pocket but with the role of the adult enabling the child to experience different learning opportunities.

Through reflection I know now that I was missing an opportunity for the children's learning. Had I been more engaged, I could have enabled the children in my care to experience more than enjoyment. Bruce's (1997) approach suggests to me now that what I was actually doing then was constraining the children's play, and because of this the 'interface and integration' experienced by the child and adult could have been more equal. I did this unwittingly. However, although the children's learning could have been deeper, early enjoyable stories from the bag helped children to make sense of what was happening in their community. There were times when, without realising it, I created what Whitehead (2010) describes as a 'community narrative'. I can see this in retrospect, but I did not know this at the time.

I had recently married. The bag contained two rabbit puppets, the book *The Rabbits' Wedding* (1973) and my wedding ring. I had left nursery on Friday, married on the Saturday and was back to nursery again on the Monday. Two children engaged with the story of the wedding and using the rabbit puppets acted out the book as the story unfolded. Gussin Paley (2014) describes the scripts children use and how they are fluid and ready to be revised during the activity. At the end of the story, John-Paul dipped his hand into the bag to retrieve the last prop – my wedding ring. He was aghast. "The rabbit's ring!" he declared. When I explained that like the story I had actually married at the weekend, he was incredulous, saying, "Eh, you are just kidding". He had, throughout, been closely engaged with the story. The atmosphere and the way the story was delivered gave the children an imaginary story which echoed a real story. This was the beginning of my use of the bag in a less didactic manner in each of the early childhood settings I have worked in.

The Froebelian principle of the adult as a gardener is a metaphor (Froebel in Lilley, 1967:93) which particularly spoke to the era in which he lived. Reflecting on this I have always felt that I garden children, enabling them to learn and be the people they are destined to be. In the current context, Bruce (2005:2) informs us that until we know the 'lenses' through which we view the child we will not achieve synergy of practice. This is particularly true when working as a team. It is important to know how colleagues working as a team view the child so that individual strengths can be used together in achieving a synergy of practice.

During group time the children requested the story bag. It is Millie's turn. She delves her hand into the bag. Millie (4 years old) says, "Ouch! Something bit my hand!" The children laugh in anticipation of what Millie might say or do next and what may be in her hand when she brings it out of the bag. They are familiar with how much she enjoys the drama of the situation. She shows everyone the 'magic bow'. The bow is a pink and sparkly brooch. Millie is delighted with this find and immediately puts on the brooch, ready to tell her story. At the time of her telling the story, I scribed for her as follows:

> Once upon a time, when there were princesses living in the palace they all decided to play in the garden. Belle was the chief princess and she led all the others out to play in the palace garden. They were putting a picnic out on the ground and all had something to eat. One of the princesses was in the kitchen to make the feast and they all enjoyed it. They were eating ice-cream and chicken nuggets. The magic bow took them to a hot place. When it was time they all had a swim in the pool to cool off. Ariel was in the water for the longest she was showing off her swimming and all the princesses clapped.

Throughout the story the children were nodding in agreement and were totally quiet, listening intently. When Millie got to the bit about Ariel showing off her swimming, the children were waving their own arms, showing Millie their own swimming strokes.

> Then the king in the palace came to see what all the noise was about. He was very cross and told the princesses to go home to get dried. The princesses all walked home in a straight line laughing. By the time they got to the palace they were all dried and happy. The king was pleased and smiled at them. The end.

Millie was an experienced storyteller. On this occasion, contrary to the usual practice, she requested that she keep wearing the magic bow. Millie went to the role-play area with her friends, and the 'magic bow' story unfolded.

After discussion as to where the picnic area should be, the children made the decision it would be in the wooden block area. Scarves were laid on the ground for picnic rugs with the girls sitting on the rugs chatting. One girl who was not with the original group had the idea to make a wall with blocks for the palace kitchen. The girls then set about building a wooden block wall, making a kitchen area. Millie then asked me if they could change where the palace was. After this the play changed dramatically as more children joined the group. The furniture from the house area was moved across the room to a new house. All that was left in the house corner was the bed. This had proved too heavy for the children to move. The drama now changed from the princess picnic to moving house. The children worked as a team moving the heavier items, listening to each other and following instructions. When they tried to move the clothes rack, it took quite some manoeuvring to get it into place.

Once the house was moved, the house corner became the palace swimming pool. Millie immediately said that the bed was the diving board and the blue carpet was the pool. Next the children demonstrated their swimming strokes. This play continued until home time. By then the whole room had become the palace and the play had transited from the original story to incorporate other agendas. However, having photographed the cooperative play scenario (with the permission of the children involved), there later followed a fascinating staff discussion about what constitutes rich play (Bruce, 2005:2) and its links to storytelling.

The content of the story was fluid and ever changing. This chimes with the views of Moss (2014), who explores how experimentation is a vital process in the development of our early childhood experiences for children. There was experimentation through negotiations during the play, and, more important, they were able to listen to views of the others who were involved.

Moss's work explores how this form of deep experimental play encourages children to become more confident. He explains how changes can come about through democracy facilitating experimentation which in turn changes relationships within the nursery community. Reflecting on this, I connect with Hardy when she espouses

> but the virtue of the real kindergarten as Froebel conceived it lays not so much in a system of occupations as in an atmosphere. (1913:83)

The atmosphere in the nursery at this moment was one of excitement, expectation, experimentation and democracy with potential for play.

Sutton-Smith (1997) asserts that imaginary play is the 'most ambiguous' type of play. What he also notes is that imaginary play is the most complex form of play and can only really be understood individually by the players. Sutton-Smith (1997:132) is critical of Froebel's principles, suggesting that his observations on play were that play was 'only

Figure 6.1 Discussing the swimming pool the children have created.

for children'. His discourse differs from Froebel's in that he omits the recognition of the Froebelian principle that the adult is a learning companion. During this play session in nursery, I was a learning companion for the children, facilitating their play and encouraging democracy in decision making, which affords ownership to the players. Trevarthen summarises this succinctly, advising that

> play may be a paradox to play theorists, but to good friends, it's a sure thing. (Trevarthen, 1997:127)

This connects to Moss's assertion that a willingness to try something new is the beginning of experimentation in the nursery. This then inspired me to explore in practice 'democracy and experimentation', creating the environments necessary for new ideas to flourish and looking at the vital role of the adult companion. The setting was a private nursery with 25 children from 3 to 5 years in age. My previous emphasis in using the story bag had been centred on the children's enjoyment. I now wanted to examine how this shared experience between props, children and adult companion affects imagination and how the environment has a crucial role to play.

Before my initial visit, I realised that I would need a conduit in addition to the story bag. This was because it was the first time I would be using the story bag with children I did not know. To bridge this gap, I used an owl puppet. The puppet introduced the children to the contents of the story bag. The owl facilitated an instant attachment with the children as they connected with the owl. This was the beginning of imaginative play with the owl.

A small group of children were engaged in listening to the owl and the things it could find in the story bag. The owl explained about the bag that contained 'all manner of magic and wonderful things', shaking the bag so that the children could hear the contents. The owl then removed the contents of the bag, which were fossils. The fossils incited much discussion about what they were. At the end of the session, the owl was quite upset at having to leave the children, flying in and out of the bag and waving to the children. The children reciprocated by waving back. The owl left the fossils with the nursery children, enabling them to explore them further.

Alison, the owner/head teacher, encouraged the children to explore the fossils and to continue to enjoy the owl during the next week in the nursery. The interest taken by children was evident, with child-initiated drawings of owls and a dedicated area where the children could examine the fossils closely with magnifying glasses. This immediate connection with the puppet illustrates the power of props in storytelling. The owl is part of the world of make-believe, which is an essential ingredient in all stories, drama and other forms of imaginative play. Reflecting on the work of Gussin Paley (2004), Lee (2016) and others suggests what the owl brought to the storytelling was 'a sense of anticipation'. The children were intrigued by the owl and its antics.

Although this was an informal project, I entered into it using some of the formal recommendations for qualitative research given by Tisdall, Davis and Gallagher (2009:55). They suggest that as 'part of a multimedia approach', props (in this case a story bag and owl) can be part of a combined triangulation (e.g., drama, children's own stories and stories that adults tell children). I used these to investigate and highlight the value of props in enabling an environment which encourages children to become storytellers who can act out and also write about their stories.

On the next visit, the children enjoyed telling the owl what they knew and had learned about fossils. The owl helped facilitate this by flying around and sitting on the children's shoulders, indicating that they would be the one to tell what they knew about the fossils. The children explained that the fossils the owl had brought in were from a sea, a long time ago. They used to be shells and corals. The children then all chose a fossil and explained a bit more about it – smooth, rough, sharp or rounded.

This session took place in the small room of the nursery as it gave more room for developing ideas and afforded the children the opportunity to join in or not. Fluidity is crucial to all young children's learning, and if the environment is not right for them at that moment in time, then learning will not be consolidated. In detailing this, Schultz (2015) advocates that the practitioner listen in order to develop a pedagogy of trust. It is incumbent on practitioners to include active participation as a mechanism affording the child choice. It is necessary to identify techniques which enable children to be motivated through their own exploration of learning. Froebel also engaged with this form of learning, and through his own personal observations he encourages us to be keen observers. One of the main principles of Froebelian learning is that of the adult role:

> The true educator and teacher have to be at every moment and in every demand two-sided. He must give and take, unite and divide, order and follow; he must be active and passive, decisive and permissive, firm and flexible. (Lilley, 1967:55)

As my visits working in the nursery continued, the children told ever more elaborate stories to the owl about their knowledge of the fossils. There was a core of six children who stayed for the whole session while others dipped in and out. Some children were content to watch while sitting or standing in the doorway. Olivia's story and picture demonstrate her engagement:

> I was with owl and then we found this sea shell and we decided to dig it up. We found other shells they were sparkly. There was only 2 shells and only 2 flowers the sand and us digging. Owl said

Figure 6.2 Olivia has drawn the owl who visits the nursery.

"Stop" I can see more shells and we both were digging very fast. I was hot. I had a dream that I could see shells everywhere even in my bed! Then we went and played in the water Owl saw shells but they weren't really shells they were other things that you find at the sea side – like fossils or very hard shells. The water was warm and I was swimming in my dress – it soon dried. Then the next day we went swimming again and I was hungry and had to eat food.

At the end of this session, the owl explained to the children that the next time it came to see them it would have very different 'stuff' in its magic bag. This created just the excitement I wanted.

The bag contained lots of different stories and drama props. One of these sessions took place outside in the nursery garden. The children took turns dipping their hands into the bag, retrieving items. By the time all the children had a turn, there were lots of props being explored by the group. Gus picked out a panda, puppy and pirate. It was completely by chance that they all began with P. He told this story. At the time of his telling this story, Gus's little brother was finding it hard to settle in the nursery.

> Panda and Puppy they were nearly the same colour that is why they are friends. They both begin with p so does pirate but he is not in the game. The puppy likes to be cuddled by the panda and the panda looks after him. They sometimes fight but mostly are friends.

Nicolopoulou (2007:267) suggests that pretend play with characters enables children to 'understand the role of internal mental processes'. Here, Gus is demonstrating his understanding of his brother's dilemma.

He then chooses a lion from the bag. "Lion and pirate – they were at sea then the lion became hungry he ate the pirate and then he wore the hat. Then he sailed to a land and found more things to eat. He was trying to eat the puppy".

"Oh no!" said two of the boys. Gus got up and led the group, running round the garden, returning to the area to find the owl for protection of his puppets. He held the owl and made it fly away from the lion with his two friends. Gus asked if he could just have the owl.

Meanwhile two more children had joined in to explore the story bag. One pulled out another panda and a baby with a crying face. One child laughed and made the sound of a crying baby. The baby was then put back in the bag and a giant knitted duck was chosen. More choices were made, and finally out of the bag there came two ducks – one blue, one yellow (the yellow one had no eyes).

> *Child:* "Why does he have no eyes?"
> *Me:* "I don't know. What do you think?"
> *Child:* "It is because his eyes are in the fluff he can see from all the bits of hair".

The child's comment indicated just how keen an observer he was. The hairstyles of today are prone to having eyes covered or partially covered by hair.

At this point an unrecognisable creature was taken out of the bag. It was finally named as a wolf. It got to work very quickly and ate everything except the panda and the owl. The owl, held by Gus, suggested a game of hide and seek by whispering in the owl's ear. Owl said to Gus that he was to hide the panda and everyone who wanted to could look for him. Gus, holding the owl puppet, was in charge. He advised the others by telling them if they were hot or cold in the search for panda's hiding place. After this game had continued for a while, Oliver asked if he could have a shot with the panda. Gus, after some thought, said, "Okay, that's cool". The game was then to find everyone, including the panda. Once the game had become more about hide and seek and not the puppets, Gus returned to a quiet area and sat engaging with the owl on his own. He asked me, "Can it just be owl and me now?" During his time with the owl, his facial expressions showed that he was speaking to the puppet. He hugged and clapped the puppet. He played on his own for a good 7 minutes until it was time for snack. Gus gave the owl back to me and enquired, "Will owl come back soon?" I said, "Yes, next week".

Donaldson (1978:121) suggests children try to make 'human sense' or 'child sense' of situations. This is evident from Gus's long discussion with the owl puppet. His facial expressions were thoughtful, pondering and at times quizzical as he used this opportunity as a personal space for reflection.

This practical work with Gus and other children has supported the need for children and adults to make the stories their own. Nicolopoulou advises that when this happens,

> pretend play, especially collaborative play, engages and pro-
> motes children's abilities to represent and coordinate multiple
> points of view and to understand the role of internal mental
> processes [and that] these skills are critical for constructing a
> 'landscape of consciousness' in narrative. (2007:267)

Analysing a 'landscape of consciousness', there are three crucial components: the role of the adult, observation and reflection.

First, the role of the adult is vital to success in connecting with children using symbols or dramatic play. The adult needs to help the children to construct images and value those that children create which are based on experiences and explain that children will use real experiences they have lived through as the basis of imaginary play (Bruce, 2005:113). Tovey advises that being a 'conversational partner' extends enquiry and curiosity (2013:114). Both these principles are key parts of learning to be a storyteller.

The story bag has been an impetus for creating imaginative play and storytelling, crucial to developing confidence and creativity in children. This coupled with the adult role defined by Trevarthen (2004:9–44) as 'learning companions' who share in the joy of play, is a force that creates an environment of deep exploration and learning for the child.

Second is the important contribution of informed observation. Drawing on the practice of Roberts (2010), I am mindful of her analysis of the purposes of observation where she gives a view from the adult's perspective, which should also be viewed from the child's perspective. It is important to do this to enable holistic practice.

Third is the need for reflection. This is a key and crucial component of Froebelian practice. It is through careful observation of the child that we can reflect on how to, in Froebel's metaphor, 'garden' and actively engage with the children in our care. This in turn enables them to grow, develop and learn in a way that engages and excites them.

Through making stories and acting out stories dramatically, the story bag I have used for 40 years can still make an important contribution to the way I work with children. Enjoyment has expanded into actively helping children to grow, develop and learn in a more holistic way, opening up new worlds of learning.

Superheroes and imaginative play

More opportunities for our children?

Deirdre Armstrong

I began this project as part of an exploration undertaken in a local authority nursery school in an Edinburgh housing estate, with 3- to 5-year-olds. In our setting, we chose a traditional story (Goldilocks and the Three Bears) to read frequently in multiple versions and observed its impact. I made a series of in-depth observations in nursery sessions over a spring term in addition to normal observations made when I was in class.

I observed Ben (4 years, 10 months), who listened attentively and enjoyed the Goldilocks story but spent almost all his time in role as a superhero. I realised he needed no roles or stories supplied by traditional tales; his imagination was fired by superheroes and *Star Wars*.

I started out with reservations about the violence in superhero play, with fears about the exclusion of girls and younger children and doubts about the nature and quality of the cartoon stories the children used as the basis for their play.

"I think *that* play is more suited to the outdoors", I would say in the face of very active superhero play, while knowing that there was another half an hour before the door would be opened to the garden. Initially I didn't take enough interest in what the play was or observe what was actually happening but simply assumed that superhero play needed space for children to move so was not appropriate indoors.

When I asked Ben about the characters he became in his role-play in the nursery, I realised how ignorant I was. As an older practitioner, brought up without a TV and seldom seeing the cartoons the children watched and played out, I had a lot to learn!

Figure 7.1 He varied his roles but usually stayed as the same superhero for several weeks, rarely playing outside his role while in the nursery.

The children in my setting were excellent teachers. Ben had been involved in *Star Wars* role-play for months while he watched it at home with his father, and he had moved into superheroes with an involvement and research into his role an actor might have envied. His clear knowledge of the characters deepened his play.

To help me catch up a bit, I found a useful book called *The Little Book of Super Heroes* which I discussed with him and other children.

I had in mind Vivian Gussin Paley's words, still so very relevant after 35 years:

> If I have not yet learned to love Darth Vader, I have at least made some useful discoveries while watching him at play. As I interrupt less it becomes clear that the boys' play is serious drama not morbid mischief. Its rhythms and images are often discordant to me, but I must try to make sense of a style, that, after all, belongs to half the classroom. (1984:xii)

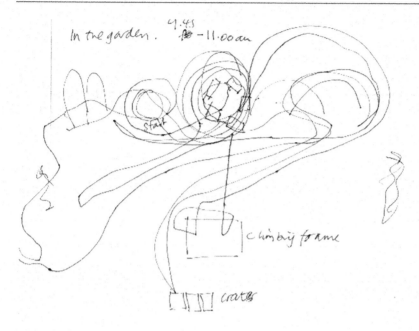

In the garden. 9.45 to – 11.00am

start

climbing frame

crater

Figure 7.2 Diagram of Ben's movement all across the garden, which became almost indecipherable as he looped and retraced his steps

Ben's superhero role took him all over the garden. He ran. "When Superman flies he goes incredibly fast, so fast he's just a blur", he said. When he chased, he was catching 'baddies' at great speed. When he kicked or beat an object, he was destroying enemies or enemy equipment: "pow!" "wham!"

Ben sometimes wore a Superman or Batman outfit, but he didn't need this to become a character; simply being in the role invested him with their powers: strength, speed, magic qualities and control of technology. In his imagination he could climb great heights, speed through the air, leap, communicate using sophisticated means, overwhelm and dispatch 'baddies' and free imprisoned people. Watching him I realised that, to him, his actions were very powerful, because Superman is invincible. In asking another child to "cut me, cut me, cut me...chop me up" and offering her a plastic saw to do it, he knew that the saw could not hurt him (as indeed it couldn't!) because he was Superman. He was, in fact, also building his own strength through such daily intensive exercise.

In his superhero role, he visibly gained confidence, either in a group or playing on his own. He was autonomous in his play choices, playing happily alongside children whose imaginative scenarios were different from his own (e.g., a child might be Skye in *Paw Patrol* while he was Batman), only requiring them to be as involved in their role as he was in his.

> Becoming a warrior or a superhero able to beat any bad guy is a generic but thrilling 'new ending' to all the everyday stories of not being old enough or powerful enough to make things come out the way children want. (Jones, 2002:67)

These superhero powers could not be summoned at all times, only when he was in role. It gave him a confidence which he did not always have as himself within the nursery setting.

Ben did not confidently take part in all nursery activities. He declined taking his turn in a singing game or answering questions when the focus was on him in a group circle, for example, preferring to offer contributions quietly when a question was asked of the whole group at story time. At the end of his time in nursery, shortly before transition to primary school, Ben had gained enough confidence in a circle game to quietly voice his name.

But in his superhero role he often led the play, choosing to play with particular children but also flexible in playing alone or with children he did not know so well. A child can never fail in acting out his role in his own drama, and this gives him a store of self-esteem which no one can take away. I began to realise that if we block opportunities for children to realise their own fantasies and dramas, we may be undermining their self-esteem.

The superhero roles which Ben chose might be male or female. He had been supported by his parents in watching films or buying props which enabled him to be in the role of Superman or Wonder Woman in a non-gender-specific way. He had regular play partners of both genders and different ages, and he drew in other children who showed themselves interested in the same characters, and some who took part without fully playing a role (e.g., in a chasing game). These dramas could be enacted by girls or boys. Penny Holland describes in *We Don't Play with Guns Here*:

> When zero tolerance (of 'warrior discourse') is in operation some boys are being prevented from exploring one avenue of gender open to them – war weapons and superhero play. (2003:20)

This can mean that they become more exclusive of girls and voice ideas that only boys can do certain things. But when

> boys received positive affirmation for interests they perceived as male some boys were able to...cross boundaries to explore areas previously considered taboo...i.e. boys can explore anything. (Holland, 2003:20)

In the play, I observed that superhero qualities and physical attributes did not necessarily need to be predominantly male. However, our reaction as practitioners to boys playing at superheroes and girls doing the same seems to be different. Generally, we feel more comfortable with girls running and chasing because we do not usually consider it to be a threat to another child. As we restrict boys' play options, girls often become aware of it and exclude boys from their play scenarios. I heard one of Ben's regular play partners saying, "The other job is to catch Romeo and only girls can do 'Romeo'" (a cartoon character in *PJ Masks*).

Girls' quieter activities are held up to be the norm, a norm which many boys do not conform to. Although girls have emerged from the 'doll corner', as Gussin Paley calls it (1984), we are not always sure about allowing their play where they become superheroes and join the boys. As Penny Holland says (2003:23), 'Girls get validation from quiet, settled cooperative activities'.

Although it seemed at times as if older children were perhaps not fully inclusive of younger ones, I began to see that there were many ways in which younger children could gain from their elders' superhero play. They could simply join in chasing or being part of a 'gang'.

I noticed that problems arose when a younger child with English as a second language was made the 'bad guy' without fully understanding his role. He had been involved in chasing games with only a rough idea of what was happening. While he didn't seem too concerned, sometimes the play became rough. I intervened, requesting that children check that others, especially those they wanted to be the 'bad guys', were in agreement with their role before involving them.

"I forgot", said Ben when I reminded him after he had taken a younger child by surprise for the second time and failed to check if he wanted to be involved. I realised then that when Ben was in role as Superman, he *had* to catch the 'bad guy' with no time to think what he should or shouldn't do.

But I needed to spend longer in observing the differences in play styles between younger and older children to understand more about the ways in which role-play can be beneficial in developing their relationships and how we can encourage this sensitively without inappropriate intervention.

In observing Ben, I began to agree with Nicolopoulou that

> young children's play narratives often begin to portray vivid, substantial and reciprocally coordinated characters before they can develop complex, sophisticated or even minimally coherent plots. (2007:261)

Ben's play was so active and at times so secretive that I could not follow his plots. They seemed to spring from his characters and what they could do. Superman can go very fast and has special powers, so the action was built on these features.

Some basic tenets of good drama were always present. Superheroes always face problems which need to be solved: "baddies" attack and need to be chased and destroyed, people needed to be rescued, a superhero needs to "save the day".

> Play is to the child a mirror of the life-long struggles that await him; therefore in order to gain strength for these, children seek obstacles, difficulties and strife in their play. (Froebel, 1826:118)

Is superhero play violent? No weapons for superheroes?

Sometimes I have not been sure whether allowing superhero play will lead to rougher behaviour where a child might get hurt. However, observation of Ben's play showed that left to themselves, he and others involved in the play found ways to use symbolic weapons but not to cause injury. Ben's mother confirmed that he often played out in the back green at home with much younger children, all brandishing 'light sabres' (sticks), and no one got hurt.

Penny Holland (2003) describes an experiment in an early childhood setting where staff took a decision to allow children to make 'weapons' and use them in play. The children fully recognised that they were 'pretend' weapons. Trisha Lee suggests that

> children are fluent in the language of pretend..."we know it's not real; we're just making up how it might be". (2016:14)

It has been argued further by Gerard Jones that the only way to deal with the complex emotions around power and violence is to play them out safely in drama so that they do not happen in real life as adults. He suggests in *Killing Monsters* (2002:67) that rehearsing themselves as powerful characters is a way to feel powerful: 'Of all the challenges children face one of the biggest is their own powerlessness'.

When I have prohibited play that involved chasing with sticks, fearing injury, have I gone further than I meant to? Holland discovered that adults' interventions did not recognise the place of fantasy in a child's life:

> Zero tolerance relies on the use of adult power in the real world to enforce a moral and behavioural imperative against powerless children operating in a fantasy world. (2003:99)

What I may have perceived as threatening to a child sometimes turned out to be a way that child was trying to join the play, for example, being chased. We need to be alert to the needs of all the children involved. I found that if I waited and listened to find out the real sources and stories in the play, I perceived the 'violent' aspects differently and found that their ways of self-regulating in their play were more effective than our own 'rules'. Using conflict in play can be a way to understand a difficult situation.

Ben's kind of play was not the same as that of a child who witnesses difficult, aggressive behaviour at home and in some way relives or copies it. Real aggression within the child's life may or may not be the trigger of pretend gun play. That play may release emotions safely or it may cause anxiety in play partners. If we suppress all weapon play, are we missing a chance for our children to express all their emotions? Could our settings provide a safe place for children to play out their difficult feelings through their own dramas? Our role is a very important one because we are in charge of maintaining this space and keeping it neutral. So we have to be very aware of how the children's dramas are developing and whether they are affecting children in different ways.

> The more a child can view the most unpleasant situations in new ways, and the more he can manipulate and dispel his most overwhelming emotions, the stronger he feels. (Jones, 2002:67)

Ben's play did not need to have weapon props, although often it revolved around play fighting. Children have always been involved in rough play, and it has had the same elements for a very long time. Blurton-Jones summarised rough play thus:

> human 'rough and tumble play'...consists of seven movement patterns.
>
> These are running, chasing and fleeing; wrestling; jumping up and down with both feet together...; beating at each other with an open hand without actually hitting; laughing. In addition falling seems to be a regular part of this behaviour, and if there is anything soft to land on children spend much time throwing themselves and each other on to it. (Blurton-Jones, 1967, in Holland, 2003:93)

I found a photo of some older children in a Benin refugee camp pillow-fighting, which showed that some of the most vulnerable children in other parts of the world, orphaned, abandoned or trafficked, still play at superheroes, finding it a safe way to express their emotions.

In my setting I began to reconsider our 'no guns, no sticks' unwritten rule and tried to carefully observe *how* the children were playing with the sticks, *what* they did with them, *why* they were part of their story and whether the 'guns' hurt other children. I realised that my questioning their self-made 'weapons' was causing children to lie to appease my worries about their play.

Gradually we began to develop a different approach to find out more from the children and ask them what was happening in their scenarios, hearing from them rather than imposing a blanket 'no guns' rule. Now I try not to prejudge the outcome of the play.

I noticed that Ben's very active play involved language – he might use the voices of superhero characters, speak into a 'phone' or describe the 'technology' he was using to a sidekick, possibly inventing words as he did so. When other children wanted to join his play, some of them simply announced the character they wished to be. Ben preferred them to be active *and* talk back in role. He liked their characters to be articulated. Sometimes this part of the play required a lot of communication and negotiation with allies – in this way I observed how he helped the language development of younger children with less advanced verbal skills and also honed his own. Ben held many stories in his head which he could draw from or use to initiate the play which enabled others to take part.

Ben drew in other children by inspiring them to take on roles. I observed Ian, a younger child (3 years, 11 months), using a robot voice – 'Master. – my master. – master. – wait. – there' – to reply to Ben when they were holding imaginary communication equipment in their hands. The younger child seemed to take on the language of a character to go with it, taking his cue from Ben, his play partner, for actions and voices. But his role would not always be subsidiary – new plot lines or whole new departures could appear when other children suggested them: "Let's go for a walk, dinosaur", said Ian to Ben when various Superman scenarios hadn't been working out.

Do superheroes need costumes and props?

Ben's play did not need many props, perhaps a stick or a stone found outside or a hat to hang out of his pocket to represent a lasso. Any props he needed were found in the moment. Ben's mother told me that he had several *Star Wars* plastic 'light sabres' which he had been given as presents but he could pick up sticks, twigs, lollipop sticks or skewers for the same purpose with no perceivable difference in the depth of his role-play. A paperclip could be a 'laser', a piece of bark a 'phone'.

Are we being too literal when we seek to extend children's play scenarios by adding an eye patch or a cloak for a pirate? In seeking to support children's play, do we sometimes substitute our own weaker imaginative scenarios?

The areas Ben chose to play in are those which have open-ended possibilities for role-play like the block-play area, the water, the sand, the house corner, places with undefined materials described as 'loose parts' by Casey and Robertson (2016: 5). Above all, he played outside in the garden. In general he avoided areas with adult involvement (for example, preparing a snack).

How can we help the children develop their stories?

In my setting the children already knew how to be in a 'stage' space, because we had already acted out traditional stories with adult support. They also knew how to become an audience and how to wait their turn to be one of the actors. This context seemed a good starting place to follow up Ben's and other children's interest in superhero stories. It seemed a way to share with a larger group some elements of the stories acted at speed in the garden.

Vivian Gussin Paley developed a practice of setting up stage spaces in nurseries where children acted out their own stories, taking the lead from the children's own imaginations (1981; 1984; 1990). I felt inspired by this and also consulted the very helpful and clear guidelines and examples given by Lee (2016), based on working with Gussin Paley.

I set up scribing and acting out a story from Ben in a story time session with a small group. I asked him to tell me a story about superheroes, which I wrote down on A5 paper. This was new to both of us, so the first story dictation and acting out was an experiment.

Ben's story: 'Wonder Woman, Superman, Batman, Robin, and Awit. They went to save the world. I think they do meet the bad guys. Wonder Woman throws the lasso of truth and it catches the bad guy'.

We made a stage with a rectangle of material laid on the floor, and the children responded enthusiastically. Here was a story where the children knew the characters, their powers and the action needed better than the adult facilitator. Children also knew the possible developments. I followed Lee's (2016:42) suggestions of offering the roles in order as I went around the circle.

Figure 7.3 The children moved spontaneously, with conviction, and swiftly held their own poses

They responded to Ben's story so expressively that it was hard to call a halt! They became involved and felt that the story had not quite been given an ending. This almost created a real drama when the 'bad guys' wanted to retaliate and fight back but it wasn't in the script. I asked for an ending from Ben, who came up with "He used his baterang" (Batman's weapon), and I brought the piece to a slightly unsatisfactory close, fearing mayhem! Later referring to Lee (2016:35), I realised I needed to follow her advice and ask the author to finalise the story as it is dictated, and in the next one I wrote 'the end'!

Immediately after that first experience of Ben's story being acted out, children crowded around the drawing table instead of going outside immediately after story time, as they normally would have done. Several children used the A5 blank booklets provided there to draw their own stories inspired by what they had just taken part in. They clamoured to have their stories scribed and wanted them to be acted out. They drew pictures and asked me to write the story underneath.

These stories began to include Goldilocks alongside the superheroes in a very interesting way:

For Helen's first story, she told me each sentence to be scribed under her drawings:

> Supergirl is trying to save Batgirl and it's not working.
> Then they stole the trophy and they got blood all over their head.
> Supergirl ran away and went into Goldilocks house and she ate all the porridge.
> Still she jumped on the bed.

Helen then drew the front cover and dictated the title:

> 'Supergirl runs into Goldilocks' house. Both of them crashed'.

Goldilocks is maybe filling the role of the 'bad guy' – or is Supergirl 'bad' too? Or are their 'bad' traits their 'good' ones too in being daring and taking action? Who jumped on the bed? Was it Goldilocks or Supergirl? And was that just fun or was it exciting because it was breaking the rules? There wasn't time to find out all the answers to these questions.

Helen moved on to a slightly changed version of her story when she dictated another story to me, this time to be acted out. I wrote it on A5 paper, checking each sentence with her. Here all the characters are taking more risky action.

Helen's story told to be acted out:

> Supergirl, Batgirl and Goldilocks bumped into each other. Then they were in Goldilocks's house. They ate all of the porridge. It was in four bowls.
> They get eaten by the bears.
> Their phones get chucked in the bin.

The children acted this out with feeling. All the characters are again breaking boundaries.

Over the next few days more stories were acted out. The children were inspired by watching others and hearing their stories. Their needs and emotions seemed to be expressed naturally through the stories they made.

This was Fay's story:

> The wee kids: one is called Supergirl, one is called Batgirl, one is called Wonder Woman, one is called Superman, one is called Batman and the lion and the tiger.
>
> They all go to Goldilocks's house and the three bears are there and the three bears eat Goldilocks. The three bears come to eat the superhero kids.
>
> The children manage to escape while they (the bears) are asleep, then their parents come and take them home safe and tuck them up in their beds.
>
> The end XXX. (They kiss them goodnight.)

Bettelheim's analysis of Goldilocks is that it does not follow the pattern of an old folk tale (it is more modern, first noted in the mid-nineteenth century) and leaves the listeners hanging without a resolution when Goldilocks flees the three bears' house (1976:218). However, Fay found a resolution to her story which satisfied her need for security.

We had some practical problems in acting out Fay's story due to the large number of characters. There were so many that the action needing to take place on the small 'stage' was impeded and we didn't have enough participating children, but the children seemed undisturbed by this.

As Lee summarised (2016:23), 'Helicopter stories has to be an activity where the children can take risks and don't feel humiliated or unsafe'.

Nicolopoulou (2007:260) found out in studying Gussin Paley's methods over a 6-month period that children started to include more themes from their pretend play in their storytelling: 'Children's identification with characters whose roles they enact heightens their interest and emotional engagement in the activity'.

Ben took part in the acting out of each story scribed alongside the others, although he might have previously refused the roles in a group activity. He commented quietly before a role was assigned to him, as

Fay's story was underway, that "wee kids can't be superheroes". I took this to mean that his own knowledge of being in a superhero role meant to him that he was the full character, not a small version, not a 'child' version of it. This demonstrated to me how he immersed himself in his roles. He *was* Superman, not 'acting' as Superman.

I realised that to help him extend his story making and avoid hindering the development of his rich imagination, I needed to welcome superheroes into nursery spaces inside and outside and listen, watch and encourage their actions.

Each generation of children has different triggers for their imaginative play. It seems that we, as practitioners, struggle to keep up, needing reminders of the educational value of free play. Again and again, children, like Ben, show us their skills and learning inspired and gleaned from the world around them, yet we persist in trying to divert them towards what we perceive to be more worthy or measurable pursuits.

Froebel first observed how inventive children's play was and how much they learned from it. Perhaps we can go back to observing children's play carefully, finding ways to encourage and support it whatever its beginnings and however active and inconvenient it may be to our settings!

I'm left questioning my practice. I need to be prepared to observe play rather than rush in to interfere. If I'm worried about children becoming physically rough I could observe and think about what they are doing and try to find out why. Are they or their props actually hurting anyone? I could examine my role in sustaining and supporting their imaginative play.

Can quieter children express their emotions, be active and act out conflicts in ways that help them build confidence through 'weapons' play? In nursery I have the chance to give them opportunities to become whoever or whatever gives them the most independence, power and self-esteem. Their superhero play may be the best way to equip them for school and all its demands on their confidence. Can I support negotiation and communication skills through superhero play? Issues of consent, safety and risk assessment are all being explored. If I ban or discourage superhero and weapons play, am I sending a message to boys that their interests and stories are less important? Am I also limiting the girls who may want to play as superheroes too? How could I help children build relationships through their play? Superhero play may offer rich and deep opportunities with stories developing through this resource. Am I ignoring present-day influences on children which are their inspiration for imaginative play? I need to be more open to their interests whether they are stories about superheroes, *Star Wars*, the three bears, or My Little Pony. Could I help bring children's own stories regularly into nursery practice through Lee's *Helicopter Stories* (2016) to help explore narratives, extend verbal skills and widen their involvement in their own fantasy play?

"Fix, fix, fix –
Olav is stuck!"

8

Supporting children to tell
the story that they really
want to tell

Elaine Fullerton

Introduction

Within a Froebelian approach to play and learning there is an emphasis
on enriching the play culture.

> A literacy-rich environment of exciting stories, scripts, charac-
> ters and plots provide a shared context for children to use and
> adapt for their own play scenarios. Stories enrich play but play
> also encircles storytelling as children accumulate a bank of draft
> scripts, plots and characters which they can use in their story
> making. (Tovey, 2017:32)

The play culture within this project was enriched through storytelling and using observation, curiosity and reflection to guide
both the resourcing and the adult role, allowing play to burgeon.
The project finished with children working in pairs to make their
own short animations. The project ran from August through the
following April. Children's names have been changed to maintain
confidentiality.

The stories that children tell through their play help them to make
sense of their inner world of feelings, experiences and the resulting
beliefs that they form about what kind of world it is and where they fit

into it, what kind of person they see themselves as and what kind of person they can become. Bruce (2015) describes free-flow play as being the highest form of learning, one in which children will rehearse their future selves.

This project was based on one of the oldest local authority nursery schools in Edinburgh, with a rich diversity of families bringing a wide variety of languages and cultures. Throughout the year stories are read and retold through small-world props or the children dressing up to act out the stories. With 53 per cent of the pupils bilingual learning – new to English, at an early acquisition stage or developing competence (SEEMiS Software Stages of English Language Acquisition, normally used for primary-aged pupils) – storybooks and props have been used for 'comprehensible input' (Krashen, 1982, in Gibbons, 2009:133) and for scaffolding learning (Bruner, 1978, in Gibbons, 2002). Children understand more than they can express at these early stages of learning English, and the storytelling props and adult support allow opportunities for children to hear the repetition of language as well as opportunities to communicate for themselves both non-verbally and verbally to retell the stories.

The focus for this project, however, was different, with a wider interest in how children used the stories we told to create their own stories and narratives in play and the types and range of props developed to meet the children's needs in play. There were more opportunities for props to be moved between areas, allowing more flow-through space as the children's play developed and deepened. Against the scaffold of stories heard, props and social interaction, bilingual learning children extended their language learning as they told their own stories. Swain (2000, in Gibbons, 2009:133) emphasises the importance of 'comprehensible output', which naturally arose from this free-flow play (Bruce, 1991) with children processing 'language at a deeper level' as they expressed their own stories.

I'm a nursery teacher; however, outside the classroom I am also a play therapist, and this experience influences our classroom practice, with an interest in looking at play from a psychoanalytical viewpoint. Froebel himself was interested in looking at play from the perspective of the inner world of the child and the relationship between the 'inner world of feelings and ideas and their outer world of things and experiences, and to reflect on them both' (Tovey, 2017:126). He wrote of children making up tales and fables:

> To us who are observing him these stories vividly reveal what is unconsciously going on deep in the mind of the young story-teller. (Froebel, 1826, in Lilley, 1967:131)

These inner worlds guide the overall project. Play arising from two of the stories, *Frozen* and *Goldilocks and the Three Bears*, are written about in more detail.

Frozen

Previous attempts to extend children's play, inspired by the Disney film *Frozen*, had been unsuccessful. When songs from *Frozen* were played in nursery, the children tended to re-enact the songs, copying the expressions and movements directly from the film. It had seemed to stifle creativity rather than extend it. We were aware, however, of how influential and powerful the themes of this film are. Children often pretended to be the lead female character Elsa in their play.

We invested in a Disney *Frozen* storybook (Golden Books) and small-world figures. On the first day I reflected that the children's knowledge of the story was far deeper than my own. I spent time later rewatching the film to deepen my knowledge. The children fluidly moved in and out of the story and songs; however, with limited figures it was difficult to actually retell the story. A girl suggested that we make more figures, and the children made the marshmallow snowman and the trolls from plasticine and a sleigh out of junk, and we collected other resources from the cupboard, including a horse, boat and various loose parts that could be used to build the locations of the castle, the trolls' home and the ice palace. As a result the play transformed.

After using the book and props to tell the story at a small-group story time, the next day a 3-year-old boy, with Malay as his first language, entered shared storytelling for the first time. He had previously come over to the area with two cars and played alongside other children. He may have been observing; however, on this occasion he played with the Hans figure, riding him in the boat, in a shared play scenario with other children. It is important for all children to understand the shared play context in order to fully participate.

On some occasions children would ask me to read the story and they would act out and retell with the props; at other times children would be playing on their own, or in pairs, making up their own stories. They continued to use some language from the story as well as the props, enabling them to tell more sophisticated stories beyond their expressive English language.

A 3-year-old boy, also with Malay as his first language, put the troll into the castle and then also locked Olav in the castle. "Fix, fix, fix, Olav is stuck", he said and then proceeded to use the troll to rescue Olav from the castle.

A 4-year-old girl, Izzah, with Urdu as her first language, played on her own with the Anna and Elsa figures. Anna went to see Elsa in her snow tower. The tower then broke and Anna said, "Tower is broke now, don't worry, I'll fix it". She used Anna to fix the tower, and then Elsa was really happy. Anna asked, "Elsa let me come in, sad, it's all broken", as she knocked the tower down again. "Come on let's go to the trolls", said Anna.

These short snippets from play show the themes that children were using in their play. They were showing an understanding of character, with all the children consistently using the trolls as the characters that fixed things. Trolls were the healers, the fixers of the world – they could rebuild towers, heal Anna when she was frozen and rescue Olav when he was trapped in the castle.

> For a story to hold the child's attention, it must entertain him and arouse his curiosity. But to enrich his life, it must stimulate his imagination; help him to develop his intellect and to clarify his emotions; be attuned to his anxieties and aspirations; give full recognition to his difficulties, while at the same time suggesting solutions to the problems that perturb him. (Bettelheim, 1976: 5)

Frozen was such a story; it held their attention as well as stimulating their imagination, and the children were exploring feelings of being scared, of being trapped, of needing help, of things continually breaking around them, of things going wrong. The trolls offered the possibility of resolution in the play. This could have resonated with the children's own internal feelings and experiences of life.

Izzah often played as the character Elsa, and like Elsa she brought her creativity and enthusiasm into social play. However, when conflicts arose the play broke down. She could find herself on her own, again similar to Elsa. Elsa was learning to make sense of her own feelings in order to both control and express her power. Izzah needed to first explore and make sense of her own feelings before being able to empathise with the feelings of others. Understanding her own and others' feelings would help her to have the close friendships that she sought.

Goldilocks and the Three Bears

The traditional story was told in small story groups, reading from the Miles Kelly version as well as telling the story with props. The children then had turns to tell the story with the props or act it out. This was the rich literacy experience that provided the shared context for children to use in their own play scenarios. These props, dressing-up clothes and a role-play area set up as the three bears' house were then used in free-flow play.

The children spontaneously moved the resources between areas. They sometimes dressed up as characters as they played with the small-world props or they dressed up as the characters and took their play into the wooden block area or outdoors. This allowed children to stay in character and play out their own scenarios. I observed that children often played one particular character. A boy, the youngest of three with two older sisters, always chose to be baby bear. He continued this later in the year with other stories. He did not retell the story but told his own stories of baby bear being mothered or being lost/trapped and then rescued. A girl who had recently had two baby siblings played out the role of being the mother, and sometimes in a play scenario in which no babies were allowed.

Play offers opportunities to explore inner feelings in relation to experiences and to be in control of the play, to be able to experiment with situations, rearrange them and create alternatives, important features of free-flow play (Bruce, 1991). Children can play out inner feelings without the consequences from acting these out in real life. It is just pretend, and this play helps them to both understand and accept their own feelings. This leads onto children developing a healthy self-awareness, in which they can accept that as well as being loving they can also feel jealous. As well as feeling scared, as is explored in the following example, they can also feel brave. Jung's (1961:306) theory of self-actualisation describes the importance of this 'liberation from opposites' as does Froebel's emphasis on the 'law of opposites' in his theory of unity.

A 4-year-old girl, Penny, with English as her first language, was anxious when she started nursery. She took time to settle and liked to be close to adults. Playing Goldilocks and the Three Bears inspired her to play out another possible self, a self that was more assertive and brave. One day she dressed up as baby bear, and instead of taking on the characteristics of a baby, she took on the characteristics of a bear. A bear can symbolise power and strength as well as a mothering role with her cubs (Archive for Research in Archetypal Symbolism, 2010).

She was playing with another girl who was playing the character of Goldilocks. Penny told Goldilocks that she was not eating porridge because she liked flakes instead. Another child walked past where she was playing and she turned round to roar at him: "I'm a bear, raaaaaa!" she called out. After a while Penny, as baby bear, said, "No more! Go away Goldilocks. Have a little walk, bye". Goldilocks left the house as instructed and went to look at books. Soon Penny joined her.

Penny has turned the story around. It is not a baby bear weeping because his chair has been broken but a baby bear who is in charge of the situation. On another occasion when we were acting out the story in a structured fashion, Penny played the role of Goldilocks. Although she ate up all baby bear's porridge and sat in his chair, she would not break it. Penny often played her own stories around this traditional tale and was developing into what kind of self she wanted to be – perhaps that powerful, strong bear who was also motherly and caring.

Nicolopoulou (2007), in her research on children's understanding through the interplay of imaginative play and children's stories that are scribed and acted, proposed a dialectical approach to the cross-fertilisation between play and narrative in children's development due to the different emphasis in the early phases of pretend play and storytelling.

> The earliest phases in pretend play emphasize and encourage increasing depth and richness in character representation, whereas the earliest phases in storytelling emphasize increasing

complexity, coherence, and sophistication in plot construction and comprehension. (Nicolopoulou, 2007:268–269)

The findings from my own project were supporting the findings of Nicolopoulou. It was characterisation that children were exploring in their pretend play, and play was the integrating mechanism (Bruce, 1991) that supported all that the children were exploring and learning about, including their inner worlds.

Burgeoning play

Children need time and space and people who encourage play in order for it to flourish and develop with depth. Play needs the right circumstances, conditions and atmosphere. Then it burgeons. (Bruce, 2012:13)

Reflections began to highlight differences in children's play across different scenarios. Izzah could flourish in a structured storytelling experience; however, in free-flow imaginative play she could play in ways that others found overpowering or scary, resulting in conflict or others leaving the play. Froebel (1905:113) wrote a long list of attributes that develop from being a member of a group in play, which include 'justice, moderation, self-control, truthfulness, loyalty, brotherly love', 'firm will', 'courage, perseverance, resolution, prudence' and 'severe elimination of indolent indulgence'. He writes of the 'blossoming of minds and hearts' as children play together. The juxtaposition is that these attributes can develop from being a member of a group; however, they are also needed to become a member of a group.

'Relationships with others, both adults and children, are key to the learning process' (Tovey, 2017:126). I explored what this adult role may look like, how to enter social play without taking over or dominating it, how to adjust to the particular children and contexts.

The true educator and teacher has to be at every moment and in every demand two-sided. He must give and take, unite and divide, order and follow; he must be active and passive, decisive and permissive, firm and flexible. (Froebel, 1826, in Lilley, 1967:55)

I used my play therapy training to sensitively enter play, to give a commentary that reflected the play and underlying feelings. If the child's story, underlying feelings and intentions in play are accurately reflected, then as Landreth (2002:211) writes, there can be a feeling of 'oneness with the child, a genuine understanding, and a "living with" that transcends the circumstances of both our lives'.

At the sand tray, a group of children were playing with animals. One child had inspired whirlpool play, which in turn had been inspired by the story *Mr Bear to the Rescue* by Debi Gliori. Izzah arrived at the sand tray with two giraffes and in a loud voice declared to each child, "We don't care!" Unconsciously these words resonated with me with the words, 'The cold never bothered me anyway' in the song 'Let It Go' from *Frozen*. Elsa sings this as she leaves her family behind and goes up the mountain to where at last she can be free to express her feelings and ice power creatively. Although Elsa enjoys this freedom, she is now again isolated and deep down she longs for closeness and companionship.

Although Izzah's giraffes were saying in a loud voice that they did not care, I wondered if they really wanted to join in but were not sure how. I reflected this back to Izzah, speaking directly to the giraffes. I reflected that the giraffes were loud and sounded angry, but I wondered if they were really feeling scared and wanted to join in, but perhaps they were unsure how to. Rubin (1983:27) highlights the array of skills needed in order to establish and maintain friendships, including to enter play 'children may have to be cautious and subtle'.

Izzah invited me into the play by giving me one of the giraffes, and I was able to reflect and model the play and intentions of other children through my giraffe. My giraffe swirled around and excitedly pretended to fall through the bottom of the tray as the other animals were doing. Izzah joined in following the play of others as well as initiating her own ideas.

She later covered up the whirlpool, and as a conflict arose with another child, Izzah looked over at me. I used the signal to explain what was happening and offer a solution; this allowed the play to continue, to burgeon. Rather than supporting children's play through discussion at points of breakdown in play, I was curious about sensitively entering children's play in character so that children could experience success. Izzah truly blossomed in the group play with an adult sensitively playing alongside.

Cozolino describes how the social brain develops and that 'the self emerges from relationships'.

> When caretaking includes emotional attunement, self-reflection, and sharing about states of mind, our children learn to be better aware of themselves and include this awareness in their narratives about themselves and the world. (Cozolino, 2006:338)

When working in the early years of childhood, it is important that our relationships with children are attuned, that we help children to make sense of and understand their emotions, that we are curious about how they are feeling and have conversations about these internal states. All of this stimulates the connectivity of neural networks in the brain, which may allow for more self-awareness, emotional regulation and an improved ability to have shared play and connections with others. Children need to be able to tolerate difficult feelings, to make sense of them, and an attuned adult helps in this process. With increased self-control, children can also develop more sustained attention. All learning is interdependent. Supporting children's emotional and social development, either through their independent free-flow play (Bruce, 1991) or with sensitive adult support in their play, is vital in supporting other areas of learning.

Every child is unique, and play will vary depending on the players involved. If one child is very excited, perhaps loud and physically exuberant, play often breaks down. Sometimes a child really enjoys scary play. They may feel scared themselves and explore this through pretend play as monsters chasing and scaring others. When play breaks down, children can feel rejected, without fully understanding why the play has broken down. With repeated experiences of feeling rejected, children can begin to feel bad about themselves. It is important that children are supported to understand and express their own feelings and the feelings of others in ways that ensure success in social play.

Multimodal storytelling

One girl was often the leader in imaginative role-play; however, she was very cautious and uncertain when I asked to scribe a story for her. It may have been that she felt more self-conscious or that the story theme was too restrictive for her or that the absence of play limited her creativity. I began to wonder which learning opportunities allowed particular children to shine and which limited their expression. Gussin Paley (2005:47) writes that teachers used to wonder about what 'faults' lay 'in the curriculum (rather) than in the child', but over her career she witnessed changes away from being interested in the child and who they were and instead trying to fix the child. I realised that we could be judging a child's storytelling abilities from one particular scenario rather than from a scenario in which they truly flourished. Nicolopoulou (2007) found a correlation between pretend play and characterisation and scribing children's stories and plot. I wondered if animation could provide a context for both strong characterisation and plot.

I had been making animations for many years with children, which was always very popular and engaged the children deeply. I wanted to reflect further as to why this may be and to evaluate the growth of the children as storytellers. Izzah and Penny worked together to make their own short animation (1.03 minutes). They had initial ideas for a narrative that changed and developed throughout the process.

The story was about a rabbit and cat. Izzah made the rabbit and carrot and Penny made the cat and milk out of plasticine. They drew and cut out pictures for the background scene. They gathered resources from the cupboard, initially a small plate and cup and later, as new ideas emerged, a well. An HD webcam was connected to the computer, and Penny and Izzah made the animation by moving the characters and clicking on the computer to take photos using the application Animate It (Kudlian Software).

My role as the adult was to be curious, to ask questions (e.g., asking what they would like their story to be about), to support the social process with each child having opportunities to share their ideas and listen to each other, to remember the story as we returned to it over a series of days, to use my experience of making animations to support the children to work out themselves how they would photograph particular sequences (e.g., how the animal would need to move to look like it was eating), to support the children to find solutions themselves to any challenges that arose and to be sensitively attuned to the stories that the children were trying to tell.

After the filming was complete, the children made a title and whilst watching the film recorded the soundtrack. I made a final edit to fit the soundtrack to the film.

A transcript from the animation – The rabbit and the cat

The following is a multimodal narrative, 'The Rabbit and the Cat'. The story is told through photographing the rabbit and cat models, modelling/remodelling, positioning/movement of the characters and spoken narrative including expression and volume in the children's voices.

> *Izzah:* "My rabbit is slip in the mud and the cat just help me stand my rabbit up and he save my rabbit today". (said jubilantly)
> *Izzah:* "My rabbit is eating a carrot cos he loves the carrots". (happy voice)
> *Penny:* "My cat is drinking the milk. My cat loves the milk".
> (The children spontaneously altered their plasticine characters, adding on red plasticine to make the rabbit look scary and a sad mouth for the cat.)
> *Izzah:* "I was scared the rabbit because he is scary" (in a loud voice) "and scared and he ran away". (said sadly)
> (The rabbit chased the cat, who ran away and hid in a well; he comes out again.)
> *Penny:* "He was scared. Don't do that ever again, don't do that ever again!"
> (Penny changed the sad mouth to a smile.)
> *Penny:* "The cat was happy now".
> *Izzah:* "They dancing and they dancing together and they happy". (happy voice)

As I reflect on the film, I realise the depth of the children's understanding of characterisation, plot and filmmaking techniques. Both the rabbit and cat have animal behaviours (e.g., the rabbit likes carrots and the cat likes milk). They also both express their feelings: the rabbit feels sad, the cat feels scared and they both feel happy. They express different emotions using their tone and volume of voice. They spontaneously use animation techniques to express feelings through remodelling of their characters. Penny uses sad and happy mouths; Izzah adds red to

Figure 8.1 Cat helping rabbit from the mud.

make her rabbit look scary. There is characterisation – the rabbit is the 'scary' one and the one who gets into difficulties whilst the cat is the helper and the one who resolves conflict. Plot is developed with events clearly linked. The rabbit slips and as a result needs helps; the cat helps the rabbit. The rabbit is scary, and as a result the cat is sacred and goes

Figure 8.2 Rabbit and cat dancing together.

to hide. The cat doesn't like this and tells the rabbit to stop. There is conflict and resolution, a coherent narrative with a happy ending.

I played the role of producer; Izzah and Penny directed their story, utilising and extending their rich first-hand experience of enjoying animation. Izzah creatively introduced ideas, and the children then responded to each other's ideas as the story unfolded. The resulting animation is made in this social context, in the meeting of their inner worlds. Group play is another feature of free-flow play (Bruce, 1991) and also reinforces the findings of Gussin Paley (1990) that social interaction improved narratives. She believed that storytelling was a shared process.

The children identified with their characters. They narrate with 'my rabbit', 'my cat'. This embodied feeling of being the character may deepen the characterisation, as it is really an aspect of themselves. The rabbit was having fun chasing the cat but recognised that she was being scary and was willing to change her behaviour to be friends with the cat. Izzah herself enjoyed chasing others in play. Jenvey and Newton (2015:174) highlight the link that most researchers have found between 'theory of mind' and social competence, although they also review evidence that 'practice, social feedback and language development, and perhaps engagement in pretend play facilitates' its development. Izzah was showing more understanding of her own feelings, with direct links between feelings and events, and was developing her theory of mind to recognise and understand the feelings of others and that these may be different to her own. She would come for adult help if needed, to support her social play. Penny, in this shared process, also helps Izzah to understand another's point of view. Theory of mind can develop well in these rich first-hand experiences.

The shared process also allowed for scaffolded language learning, developing their fluency with English language. This included recording the narrative in response to feedback from each other.

Penny was a girl who had grown in confidence. She was more independent in her play and expressing herself more confidently. This is reflected in the cat's character. It is through the cat's assertion that they then decide to dance together and have this shared moment of pleasurable connection.

Mackenzie (2011:1) highlights the importance of multimodal expression once instruction in writing begins. Her research highlights the importance of 'encouraging the three modes of expressions (drawing, talking and writing) to work together' to create more complex texts than children could produce by writing alone. Cremin, Flewitt, Swann, Faulkner and

Kucirkova (2018) highlight how children co-construct stories through multiple modes using the Gussin Paley approach to storytelling including the sensitive attunement of the adult showing respect for the stories. This project also demonstrates multiple modes that children use when co-constructing stories using animation, including the adult role of showing respect and valuing the stories that the children tell.

Co-constructed multimodal storytelling did produce complex narratives and more complex narratives than either the visual or spoken narrative told on its own. The storytelling was an embodied experience as the children made and moved their characters, and the end result was a high-quality expressive narrative, demonstrating good understanding of both plot and character.

Conclusion

Stories are the purest form of self revealing. Every story you write or tell reveals you. It is impossible to conceal yourself in your stories. More revealing than the face, are the stories you tell. A story is the most self-betraying act we engage in. We are never more than in our stories. (Okri, 2015:30)

Ben Okri, the author, highlights for me the importance of the stories that children tell and the important role as adults that we have to provide children with rich literacy environments which can fuel these stories, a permissive space to tell or play their stories as well as listening and being curious about the stories that they tell and what they could be revealing to us about their inner worlds. Supporting children emotionally and socially will allow all children to flourish in their learning and also flourish in their lives.

Key findings

- Stories that capture the childhe childdabout the stories that they tell and what they could be reveal

- In a permissive environment, these stories inspire children to tell their own stories.

- Pretend play supports children to develop as storytellers.

- Children use storytelling to express their inner world of feelings and ideas outwardly. Play also strengthens and refines the inner world of feelings and the child's developing sense of self.

- The sensitive role of the adult can help play to flourish.

- Talking about states of mind is important. This supports emotional awareness, self-awareness, self-esteem and theory of mind development.

- Emotional and social developments are reflected through the stories children tell.

- Co-constructed multimodal storytelling can produce rich characterisation and complex plots and is vital for children to be able to deeply express themselves and learn from each other.

- Learning is holistic, experienced as a meaningful whole. Play is the integrating mechanism.

9 Woodland adventures

Lucy Macfarlane and Rosemary Welensky

Our study of literacy through play initially developed through our weekly Forest Kindergarten sessions. Working at one of Edinburgh's largest independent schools, we had the trained staff available to enable us to take the children outdoors regularly to our Forest Kindergarten site. In the woods, our 'carried-in' resources were limited, as we preferred to source natural objects from the forest floor. However, the bag containing storybooks came to be of significant importance to the groups of children that we took to the woodland.

> Story is a vital tool for children, for it offers a place for them to explore and make sense of the various words, sights, sounds, tastes, smells and textures that bombard their senses each day. By taking on roles in fantasy children experience different situations and empathise with the perspective of others. (Lee, 2016:58)

The book bag contained stories that shared a similar theme of nature, outdoors and adventure. We observed over many years that although we offered a choice of stories, the same book was repeatedly chosen time and time again. We both share the belief and note the importance of rereading children's favourite books. *Not a Stick* by Antoinette Portis became a staple Forest Kindergarten resource. We began to note the impact the story had upon the children's verbal communication and within imaginative role-play that occurred in the forest but which then also continued upon their return to the classroom.

> One of the best methods for gauging what a child understands about reading is to share a book and note what the child does. (Bruce, 2012:281)

Intrigued by the success of this simple book which uses minimal colours, images and wording, we began investigating why this story had such an impact on play. Froebel believed that

> the teacher's task consists of preparing the ground, setting the scene and then retiring to the periphery so as not to intervene in the learning process. (Liebschner, 2001:138)

This leads us firstly to discuss the importance of understanding the difference between telling a story and sharing a story. Over the years we have observed adults reading this same story time and time again. They have shared the children's enthusiasm and have encouraged their ideas whilst also supporting their excitement as each page is turned. However, we have also seen adults tell the story, gently explaining their adult interpretation of each image, without offering the children the freedom to use their own imaginations.

> To immobilize his (a child's) body is to silence his language and this thought. (Engel, 1995:156)

It would be our preference to share this book with the children in our groups and share their enjoyment of re-creating the story with every read.

We noted that *Not a Stick* encouraged children's participation and the use of their imagination to bring depth to the story. We saw that the joy of developing the story themselves allowed the children the freedom to decide on creative outcomes without the fear of being wrong, which was reflected in their eagerness to participate in a story. This allowed them freedom for interpretation and enabled them to take the lead in the storytelling process, and in turn this affected their role-play.

> Freedom was especially essential, for teachers and children alike, when encouraging the creative aspects in a child's development. (Liebschner, 2001:140)

First-hand experiences at Forest Kindergarten

A group of eight children were the first to visit Forest Kindergarten, ranging in age from 3 years and 10 months to 4 years and 11 months.

Five children within the group were those who had been deferred due to their birthday falling between December and February. Many of these children found forming friendships and joining group play challenging. It was our hope that during their time in the forest they might discover new friendships, strengthen existing friendships, develop in confidence and find their voice. Working with small groups of children allowed us as both a teacher and a practitioner to tune in to these children, as Kallalia states:

> Educators who do not really see the child cannot fully bear pedagogical responsibilities. (Kallalia, 2006:124; also in McNair, 2012:63)

This enabled us to observe their play, watch it grow and develop as they took on new roles and characters in the freedom of the forest.

On a cold winter's morning, we brought the children to Forest Kindergarten for the first time. We introduced them to their surroundings and gave them time to explore the forest within boundaries that were discussed and created with them. They ran around with glee, finding trees to climb and puddles to jump in, calling to others to join them in their discoveries.

> The natural landscape offers children first-hand experiences of nature where they can know and come to understand the changing seasons. There are no toys. The site itself fosters opportunities for folklore and inspiration for games of pigs and wolves and building houses to keep safe and hide from the wolves, or playing fairies and goblins, children have a wide range of opportunities to use their imaginations to convert features of the environment. (Bruce, 2012:62)

When tummies began to rumble and the children were all in agreement, we sat down for our forest snack, and much to their delight the book bag was finally opened. Within the bag we offer a selection of books that the children as a group are able to choose through a vote. It came as no surprise to us that the first story they chose was *Not a Stick*. Once the story had finished, they were immediately eager to have it read to them again, and they began to join in by recalling the words of the story and anticipating the next page's images. Whitehead writes:

Careful thought and organisation must go into the environment in which children hear stories and investigate books. (Whitehead, 2007:44)

This is a statement that we believe to be very accurate. When in a classroom, careful thought and consideration goes into making the story corner both cosy and welcoming. Outdoors, however, children have the freedom to choose where best they would like to hear a story. They have ownership of the location, and each week it has the flexibility to move to their chosen spot. After snack time we observed the play in the woods change from exploration to role-play. We noticed the key phrase being used from the book: 'It's not a stick, it's a ...' We saw the story begin to influence play. The children started to find sticks and began using the wording from the book: 'This is my "not a stick"'. Nicolopoulou states that

children's pretend play and storytelling appear to operate as parallel activities with surprisingly little thematic interchange or mutual influence. (Göncü and Gaskins, 2007:253)

We saw the children's pretend play being almost immediately influenced by storytelling. This excited us.

Recorded observations of Finlay

Finlay, one of our deferred children, was the first to re-create the final page of the book through role-play. He found a stick and immediately stated, "It's not a stick, it's a sword". Others quickly followed in his footsteps, finding their own sticks and exclaiming what they were. Finlay rounded up the other children, who joined him in becoming a knight. His 'not a stick' was his sword, and he was on a mission to protect his castle (tree) from the dragon. The rest of the group became involved within his role-play; Finlay gave each a specific role to play. The only rules were that you had to have your own stick and you had

Figure 9.1 "My 'not a stick' is a sword. I'm a knight. I need a sword so I can attack. I am going to attack bad people. I protect my castle".

to play by Finlay's rules! They each used their chosen sticks as props for the characters they had become.

When we returned to the classroom, the play from outside continued but in a different form. The boys from the group went straight to the drawing table. Finlay's imaginative role-play was carefully transferred onto paper, and from the drawing he began to naturally recount his story.

Finlay made a story: "My castle is the big tree. I can see the forest and see the baddies coming from the lookout tower. I can run out and fight the baddies with the other knights. When the baddies are killed we can put them in the deep jail so the baddies can't get out".

Play is not the only medium through which children rework a challenging story; they frequently use drawing, painting and the manipulation of materials and objects as ways of representing their thinking about experiences. (Whitehead, 2007:31)

I asked Finlay if I could photocopy his picture and whether he would like it during his next visit to Forest Kindergarten. He nodded in agreement. Inspired by Trisha Lee's approach to storytelling in her book *Princesses, Dragons and Helicopter Stories* and intrigued by Finlay's imaginative stick story, we gathered as a group and acted out his story together. Finlay was a quiet and introverted little boy. However, confidence and pride both shone through as he took on the role of a knight in front of his classmates. I invited the rest of the group to discuss their games during Forest Kindergarten. Many of the children shared full narratives about their play, whilst others found extending their conversation beyond the literal a challenge: "I played with sticks, it was a stick".

Initially Finlay's role-play did not continue when he re-entered the forest the following week, the children all delightedly explored the

Figure 9.2 The girls gathered sticks, ropes and leaves to create a dragon to scare off the boys.

trees. Their imaginative role-play diversified, but they continued to use sticks creatively. When it came to snack time it was clear that their interest in *Not a Stick* continued. Again, the children chose to read *Not a Stick* and participated even more, remembering the sequence of the story.

After snack, we could hear the wording from the story repeated through various group games.

"It's not a stick, it's a dragon".

"It's not a stick, it's a stirring spoon". (as a group of children created a mud kitchen in a large puddle)

"It's not a stick, it's a cutting machine". (as a boy plays a solitary game, using a large stick as a scythe)

Although the role-play continually changed, the wording was repeated throughout the session.

Recorded observations of Elsa

Elsa took a keen interest in *Not a Stick* during her second visit to the forest. In class, she liked to carry a special book around the room with her, asking adults to reread the story throughout the day. She took *Not a Stick* and looked through every page, retelling the story to herself. When she had finished, she noticed that on the back of the book there was a picture of another book. She excitedly pointed this out to the group, and they asked what the book was. We explained that the author had written another book called *Not a Box*. They were all interested to know more about the book and if we could bring it to share with them at Forest Kindergarten the following week.

We introduced the new book, *Not a Box*, to the whole class. We facilitated this by adding a variety of boxes, large and small, to the classroom and outdoor areas. Although the wording from the book was only repeated by one child (a child from our Forest Kindergarten group), the play with the boxes continued for days on end. And as any early childhood practitioner will be aware, the box was not, not, not ever a box!

At the next session in the forest, as requested, we brought the *Not a Box* book, but to our surprise they asked us to read *Not a Stick* first.

Once we had read *Not a Stick*, they were then keen to investigate the new book. They enjoyed meeting the new character within the story, and all joined in enthusiastically trying to guess what the rabbit was going to be using the box for.

After the book had been read and their snack was finished, Elsa asked if the lady who wrote these books had written another book. Unfortunately, she had not written a third book, but it led us to pose the question to the group. If she was going to write another book, what could she write about?

Murray was quick to answer: "Not a House?" But the rest of the group said, "No, that won't work".

Giselle said, "Not a Log?" They agreed that might work.

Another boy said, "Not a Monkey?" The other children said, "No, that won't work", but the boy said, "Yes, because monkeys can be different types". They thought about that but said nothing more.

Freddie said, 'Not a Leaf?' Everyone thought that would work.

Recorded observations of Freddie

They then went off to play in the wooded area. After 5 to 10 minutes, Freddie introduced us to the children he was playing with as Not a Stick, Not a Box, Not a House, Not a Leaf and himself. Freddie was a natural leader in play, and no matter if he was outside or in the classroom his play would attract a large group of friends to participate. During their session at Forest Kindergarten, their play continued on a large dead branch of a tree that was on the ground. We could hear them calling to each other as they played, for example, "Not a Leaf, come over here". Their play continued until the end of the session with all four children engaged in it all the time. They were disappointed when we had to head back to their classroom.

As we returned to the classroom, Freddie continued to lead a discussion about what 'not a somethings' they could become. Perhaps after their role-play they had developed more understanding that the object worked better when it was inanimate? They suggested pine cones, stones and ropes. We were keen to see where we could take this imaginative play and worried that entering the hustle and bustle of the classroom might lose the children's focus on 'not a somethings'.

Creating our own stories

We decided to stop outside and have a chat to listen and record the children's book ideas. Froebel believed that

> people, and that included children, are more receptive if they are co-operating by choice rather than participating through coercion. (Liebschner, 2001:140)

We talked further about creating our own book and had a vote on what the objects could be. The children decided that we could have more than one book and each came up with a suggestion. 'Not a Stone', 'Not a Rope' and 'Not a Pinecone' were the chosen three.

Maggie was the first one to mention characters. We found it interesting that the book they had all favoured had very little in the way of characters. The author, Antoinette Portis, has drawn the only character within *Not a Stick* as a simple outline of a pig, and the single character within *Not a Box* is again a simple outline of a rabbit. Our discussion took a different turn, and whilst we entered and changed out of our waterproof suits, the children began to argue over the book characters. To stop the arguing, we suggested that we have a group time to make up characters for our new stories. The children were enthusiastic, and all sat down once they were changed. Again, each child created a character, and we went to a vote to choose the top three. We had a dog, a polar bear and a fox.

Our story – 'Not a Stone'

> Two characteristics are fundamental – confidence and joyousness in telling stories. (Engel, 1995:207)

Prior to visiting the forest for one last time, with the help of the children, we made three book covers, created in a similar style to the Antoinette Portis books, using the children's chosen characters. We looked at all of the book covers and chose one to talk about first. The children chose 'Not a Stone'. Using a basket of random stones, I asked the children each to pick their own 'not a stone'. We closed our eyes and thought about our stone. Then we each took a turn to show the group what our stone was.

Finlay said, "It's not a stone, it's a skateboard", and he stood up on his stone.

Elsa stated, "It's not a stone, it's a baby, shhhh!", and she rocked her stone gently.

The other children made mountains and elephants and other imaginative suggestions. We repeated all their suggestions back to them and told them that they had made a story. The children seemed quite pleased, and we headed off to the forest.

> The act of telling the story is important for children to develop a love of relating stories and for giving them a full sense of the range of narrative possibilities. (Engel, 1995:168)

Our final visit to the forest

The children played amongst the trees, and we noted that their play did not relate to our group time discussions or any of our stories. At snack time we sat down and chose our books. This time the children asked for *Not a Box* first, followed by *Not a Stick*. Afterwards Freddie recalled our stone story. "Why are you sniffing that stone?" he said in the voice of a character. "It's not a stone, it's a flower". The children began to giggle, and each began to create their own versions of the story again.

> *Finlay:* "Why are you sitting on those stones? It's not a stone, it's a chair".
> *Freddie:* "It's not a rope, it's a zip wire".
> *Giselle:* "Why are you piling up those stones?"
> *Maggie:* "Why are you rocking that stone?"
> *Mark:* "Why are you stroking that stone?"
> *Elsa:* "Why are you standing on that stone? It's not a stone, it's a surf board".
> *Murray:* "Why are you sliding about on those stones? It's not a stone, I'm skiing".

When they had finished their snack, the call of the trees was too great. One by one they left the snack area. Finlay, the leader of the group, went back to his favourite tree, picked up a stick and shouted to the girls,

"I'm a knight, and I'm going to attack". The girls made off to the opposite tree. They collected sticks and used rope to make a dragon to trap the knights. The boys attacked using their stick swords, and the girls screamed and roared as dragons. All too soon their forest adventure was over and we returned to the classroom, many clutching treasured objects found on the forest floor.

Cleave and Brown suggest that

> four-years-olds need space as they are very active, both physically and mentally, and also because their motor development is at a crucial stage. (Cleave and Brown, 1991:5)

Taking a small group of children to Forest Kindergarten and using it as our environment to study how literacy affects play has enabled us as adults to stand back, observe, record and support children's play when necessary. But most importantly it has given the children space, time and freedom to fully explore their interests without the bustle and noise of a classroom environment.

After 4 observational weeks in the forest with one group of children, our aim was to discover how their interest in the *Not a Stick* story and their play would correlate and whether they would continue to develop the theme of their play further each week. We witnessed their imaginative forest games leave the sanctuary of the woods and return to the classroom, taking on new life through drawing and storytelling. Through further observation and researching the literature, we hoped to support the children in creating their own stories and books in the form that they decided on, within the environment of outdoors. We wanted to observe how the children's storytelling would develop through transition to Primary 1.

Since our study and research, we have introduced a literacy shed to our outdoor area, where we have placed copies of our favourite stories, including *Not a Stick* and our own children's stories, to enable literature to be accessed at all times. The shed has been incredibly popular, and our books have never been muddier.

With the success of Finlay's *Not a Stick* story together with being inspired by the teachings of Trish Lee and Vivian Gussin Paley, we were encouraged to attend Trisha Lee's training in helicopter stories. Since then we have implemented her approach in our weekly timetable, offering protected and quiet time to enable children to tell their stories. We share and act out our stories on a weekly basis and have observed a wonderful increase in both children's storytelling confidence and in their self-confidence when performing in front of their peers.

We have witnessed the shyest of children grow from being observers to performers, and it has led us down a new avenue of exploring our practice. Is there a difference in the stories that children tell when they are outside, when inspired by natural objects around them in comparison to storytelling in a classroom environment?

We realised that the location where children shared their stories was of vital importance. Storytelling in the midst of a loud and bustling classroom often led to stories that were simplistic: "I went to the shops with Mummy to get stuff for tea. Daddy likes chips and Mummy likes potatoes"; "I stayed in a hotel. I stayed in a hotel with my mum, my dad and my brother. I stayed in the hotel and it had a swimming pool. We went to a park. The hotel was big and my room had two bed in it".

Whereas sharing stories outdoors often led to children using their surroundings to support their imaginative storytelling: "Once upon a time there was a magic tree"; "There's a rainbow house".

With helicopter stories now fully implemented in our daily nursery life, we began to observe children's play after they had shared their stories. Their characters would often come to the forefront of their games, allowing their stories to come to life through play.

The children's love of storytelling often surfaces throughout the day. Even whilst adventuring in Forest Kindergarten, one of the children might ask to tell us a story. We have begun to factor in storytelling into our Forest Kindergarten experience and now always ensure that our story bag is also equipped with pens and paper for jotting down their imaginative tales. However, as much as they enjoy sharing their stories at Forest Kindergarten, they never choose to act them out in the woods, always saving them until they return to their classmates.

Transition to Primary 1

The children have now moved through to Primary 1, the first stage of more formal education, but they are still being taken out to Forest Kindergarten. We thought it would be interesting to see how and if their interest in the *Not a Stick* book would remain. At the time of the observation below, they had been on holiday from school for 7 weeks and also been in Primary 1 for a term of 16 weeks.

Observation 1

In this first group, there were only a few of the children mentioned previously, two children new to the school and the remainder who also moved through from our nursery. Play started with exploring the area and climbing trees and staying very much with the group. When snack time was decided, we offered the children a choice of three books, including *Not a Stick*. The vote was for *Not a Stick*. The new children were told by the existing children that this was a good book and that they would like it!

Once we started to share the story, the children who were familiar with it excitedly called out, "It does say not a stick!" They enjoyed being able to read the text in the book and being able to confirm that it said exactly what we had read to them previously when they were in nursery.

Reading is about investigating print and recreating the message it carries for our own purposes. (Whitehead, 2000:2 February)

They remembered the story content well and were very pleased when they guessed the next page before we read it together. We were amazed by how much they had remembered and how much of their own additions and thoughts they had remembered too after a long summer holiday and a term in Primary 1. The new children quickly picked up the thread of the story and were happy to add their own unique thoughts too.

After snack, all the children played together, often using the 'it's not a stick, it's a ...' phrase from the book. We noticed that their play seemed deeper and more complex in their imaginative ideas and concepts. They really were not keen for the Forest Kindergarten session to finish and always asked when the next session would be.

Observation 2

This book continued to be the favourite with other books only being considered after *Not a Stick* had been shared. It was interesting to us that even when other books were shared, none of them seemed to have the impact that *Not a Stick* had, and this included the children new to this story.

The children expanded their play in the forest using their 'not a sticks' for a variety of imaginary scenarios. Sticks could be large and small; for example, a large log with five children sitting across became 'this is not a stick, this is a train', and smaller sticks became 'this is not a stick, this is a Y'.

Conclusion

One of the most important messages that has come from our observations is that once children have the confidence to voice their opinions and ideas, they blossom. Certain buffers have to be in place; for example, they need to see that anything is okay. Your story is 'your' story and therefore never wrong. Any story is shared and not just 'read', and there is no rush or timescale for this story to start or end.

> The fact that young storytellers are smack in the middle of a love affair with this powerful new world of words means that, if encouraged in the slightest, they will relish the words they use and be eager to experiment with new ones. (Engel, 1995:156)

We have had 100 per cent participation eventually, and this includes children who rarely speak in nursery. We feel that again certain buffers need to be in place for this to happen. These are being outside in a 'wilder' space than the nursery garden and in a small group. Each session should be child led and child centred so that the children realise that they are important members of the group and will be listened to. The group becomes a small community in which adults and children support and know each other. Once children feel nurtured and 'safe' ('safe' encompasses a huge range of things), they can relax and enjoy the community and all the wilder space can offer them. Literacy comes easily if all these are in place.

Key messages

We think the most interesting questions that have come through these observations are the following:

What makes the children choose the same book each time?

How important is the content, graphics, text and subject?

Is the choice of the same book linked to the interests and point in development of the child?

If the children developed their own book, would they choose this book each time?

Will the sharing of the same book each time encourage an early love of reading?

The stories children tell us about their transitions from early childhood settings to primary school

Lynn McNair

With storytelling as the focus, this chapter will address the importance of early childhood transitions, drawing on an ethnographic study. This demonstrates how, when there are disruptions in the early childhood journey, children struggle. In most parts of the world, early childhood is regarded as being from birth to 7 years. If on entry to primary school their experience is such that they find it difficult to build on the 'story' learning they have begun to develop, much will be lost and delayed. Mental health and well-being may be affected, and behaviour issues may arise. Transitions are important. They need to help rather than constrain the learning of young children.

Introduction

Human beings may see the caterpillar's metamorphosis into a butterfly as a thing of great beauty; however, perhaps, for the caterpillar it is a traumatic experience – maybe it thinks it is dying. Early childhood practitioners and parents and caregivers want the transition to be a positive experience, and not a traumatic one. This chapter explores

Figure 10.1 Tilly before starting at school.

the stories young children (our caterpillars) share about their journey as they transition to school. Sands (2012) reminds us that 'stories have been told ever since we could scratch marks onto cave walls. Stories have been powerful forever, across all cultures, all time. The ones we remember are the funny, sorrowful, poignant, bumpy, joyful ones that capture our hearts and minds. They connect the past and future, into the present, and make us remember; let us imagine; create other worlds; other identities' (Sands, Carr and Lee, 2012). This ethnographic study is an examination of the, at times, poignant, bumpy stories of 16 young children as they metamorphosis from an early years centre, Lilybank, to four primary schools, Northfield, Southfield, Eastfield and Westfield, in one Scottish city. 'In its literal translation, the term "ethnography" means writing about people and ... that it is the use of ethnography as a research methodology which has enabled children to be recognised as people who can be studied in their own right within the social sciences. In this sense ethnographic methods have permitted children to become seen as research participants and, increasingly therefore, it is ethnography which is fast becoming the new orthodoxy of childhood research' (James, 2002:246).

I had a long-term relationship with the children who took part in the study, some of whom I had known for 5 years. All the children attended the early years setting where I worked for 13 years. In some cases, I had known many of the parents for longer, as elder siblings had also attended the centre. Mandell suggests such relationships are crucial in unearthing hidden information, and other writers argue that an ethnographic approach is the most effective methodology for this kind of study.

> To carry out research with children does not necessarily entail adopting different or particular methods ... like adults, children can and do participate in structured and unstructured interviews, they fill in questionnaires; and on their own terms, they allow the participant observer to join with them in their daily lives. Thus, although some research techniques might sometimes be thought more appropriate for children, with regard to particular research contexts or the framing of particular research questions, there is, we would argue, nothing particular to children that makes the use of any technique imperative. (Christensen and James, 2001:2)

Therefore, in order to capture the children's stories of their transitional experiences, I was not restricted by particular methods, and I did not only consider methods that were considered child methods; I was interested in what the children wanted to share. For example, as well as mind-mapping sessions and informal chats, some children drew pictures that they thought I would be interested in, sharing stories as they expressed their thinking (Wright, Diener and Kemp, 2013).

The data showed that *power* was a central concept in understanding transitions. The voices of children were often silenced by

Figure 10.2 Tilly depicts children sitting at desks in school.

policymakers, bureaucrats and professionals during the process or overshadowed and undermined by mainstream procedures. Children were expected to become acquiescent, adjusting to coercive practices used in the school institution. However, the findings also showed that some children observe ways to creatively resist organisation. The stories of children can (and do) add nuance to our understanding of how power affects their transition experience.

The early childhood context – Lilybank

The early childhood setting was rooted in the principles of Friedrich Froebel (Froebel, 1887; Bruce, 2012; Tovey, 2017). Consequently, childhood was viewed as a powerful concept (Bruce, 2012; Bruce, 2015;

Bruce, Hakkarainen and Bredikyte, 2018; McNair in Bruce, Elfer and Powell, 2019). The idea of 'childhood' (what is a child?) varies widely. The view held at Lilybank was that children are competent beings who are able to act in and interpret the world around them. However, importantly, early years practitioners (EYPs) stressed that no two children are the same. The idea that EYPs could have a single understanding of the child ignores the significance of movements and migrations to children's lives, the profound differences between children attending the multiethnic centre, in terms of gender, age, ability and religion. At Lilybank, EYPs could often be heard saying, "We *live* alongside our children" (Froebel, 1887). Inevitably, the EYPs accepted that children had different competencies. Furthermore, at Lilybank, the EYPs did not use the labels often used in other settings to identify the different children they worked with (e.g., infants, toddlers, tweenies, preschool children or primary school-aged children), nor did they stratify children according to their age (Bruce, 1987). At Lilybank, children freely used the spaces available to them. Thus, it was quite a liberal environment. As Tovey stressed,

> nurseries and schools should be democratic, respectful communities, where adults and children learn from each other. (Tovey, 2017:3)

Subsequently, children were not 'taught' by adults with goal-orientated plans; rather, learning was child led. Children were educated in the spirit of critical democracy, knowledge, passion and social responsibility. Importantly, children were trusted to take risks (Lahno, 2001). Froebel focused on the benefits rather than the risks. He recognised the sense of joy and freedom associated with pushing the boundaries beyond the limits of everyday experience.

> Froebel also argued that children who experience increasing challenges in their everyday play were safer than children who have been protected from them. (Tovey, 2017:72)

Consequently, children were enabled to challenge themselves but were also challenged by highly skilled adults.

Mind mapping – children claim their moral and political agency

The children's experience of transition was 'unknowable' – a subject for hypothesis – the vital distinction between the world as it is in itself and the world as it appears to us. Mind mapping was a tool that was used in the early childhood settings to explore children's thoughts, stories, feelings and suggestions. Mind mapping provided an opportunity for the children to answer a question, and then children's responses were captured in a visual way.

The area where mind mapping took place was a safe and familiar environment to the children (Lahno, 2001). This was a space where the children's views were sought, more formally, on matters that concerned them. The mind-mapping sessions that took place from April to June told us so much about the children's hopes, fears, aspirations and desires, for example:

Hopes: "I'm going to [name of school], and I might see Lewis there".
Fears: "I'm a wee bit scared".
Aspirations: "When the snow comes I might ask if I can play ice hockey", "I might write for the first time without my dad".
Desires: "I am looking forward to going to school, but I think school should be in Lilybank. Primary 1 should be in the [name of a space] at Lilybank", "I would like to read". (mind-mapping session, May)

Mind-mapping sessions were guided by the children's stories (Puroila, Estola and Syrjala, 2012). The children were used to being listened to responsively and were comfortable speaking their body-minds. The children sat in a circle so that they could see each other's faces. Their philosophical points were recorded. These sessions signalled to the children that their stories mattered. Giving children the opportunity to tell their own stories enabled them to make meaning and gave the EYPs an insight into their current thinking. Writing down their stories or views made it less likely that they would be forgotten, and therefore (arguably) children had more agency than if the stories were only spoken. In this setting of more or less self-sustaining democratic practice, the children learned to take risks in dialoguing that was permissible and valued. When the children were consulted about going to school, at the early stage their responses were close to the experiences they had at nursery. For example, when the children were asked what they would like to do at school, they mentioned 'play'.

I could tell from the children's expressions who had more experience of school than others. For example, one boy was already at the school nursery, and he was able to tell stories through attending the large school assembly. As Holland, Reynolds and Weller argue,

> children use resources and networks to negotiate a move to a new school and become social actors who are able to settle in and 'get on' .... Networks of friends, acquaintances and siblings help them to become familiar with the school, find their way around, learn the unwritten rules and practices, and to become confident and settled. (Holland, Reynolds and Weller, 2007:101–102)

Fabian and Dunlop (2007) and Moska (2010) put forward similar arguments. The mind-mapping settings set in train a process that revealed other stories that the children were keen to share:

> "Guess how old I am!" Superman asked excitedly. Superman looked at me smiling, hardly able to contain the answer. I have a puzzled look as if I don't know or can't guess; all the while knowing she had a big birthday party at the weekend. A small hand appears from behind her back holding five fingers widespread. "Five", I answer. Superman squeals with delight. "When did that happen?" I ask. "I am five now, I had my birthday [party]". The birthday party signifies this is indeed so. "I am going to school soon. I am going to the same school as my sister". I smile and agree with Superman as she stands there in her sister's hand-me-down school uniform, a grey pinafore and white short sleeved blouse, clearly delighted at bringing me this exciting news. (Lilybank field notes, May)

Some children easily accepted that they would move to school. Above, Superman prepares for school and begins to leave behind the previous phase of her life. Superman looked forward to exploring the new space (Moska, 2010). Her status was changing, although she had not yet assumed her new identity of being a schoolchild. She had already begun to display identification with her soon-to-be school by wearing her (borrowed) school uniform. This opportunity to dress up offers a unique opportunity for Superman to develop and exercise her agency, identity and voice. Reaching school age is evidently worthy of celebration to Superman. Going to school was already something Superman knew a lot about as she had an elder sibling (Mina) already at her primary. From Superman's story, it becomes clear that she had begun to own the ideas and beliefs of her culture and she had embarked on her journey, making sense of her world through interactions and activities (Rogoff, 2003).

For many children like Superman, reaching school age signals a time of 'getting bigger'. However, not all children celebrate their age in the same way. Just because a child turns 5 does not mean that they automatically feel prepared for school, nor that they have the social resources to draw upon to negotiate the passage (McNair, 2016). Some children expressed their dilemma at reaching school age. Omar (who had no older siblings) said, "I don't want to go to school. I am too little to go" (Lilybank field notes, May 2012). Omar was a tall boy and bigger than many of his peer group. It is unlikely that he perceived himself as too small physically; rather, he felt too young to go to school. Intended to define his soon-to-be 'school life', Omar was given the message from his parents that 'big boys' go to school (Majanovi-Umek, Fekonja-Peklaj and Polesek, 2012; Lilybank field notes, May 2012). Omar's reality, however, was quite different, and amongst the children who participated in the study, his perception was not unique (Khimji and Maunder, 2012).

As the time for going to school drew closer, another mind-mapping session, in June, revealed that the children's stories illustrated an understanding not solely of the knowledge required when starting school (e.g., literacy and maths) but also of the values that underpin the school and the compromises they may need to make with regards to the notion of participation. Children started taking school more seriously. From the children's stories, they had begun to appreciate the more formal behaviours of schoolchildren. "You have to listen to the teacher". "You have to wear a uniform". Their stories included knowledge of where they would be positioned in the school:

Paloma, 4 years: "When the adult is reading a story, you need not to speak".
Me Me, 4 years: "When the teacher tells you to sit down, you cross your legs. But the teachers don't actually read the children learn".

Sweety, 4 years: "When you are having a story, you have to be very quiet because the children are reading. You read and write".

Natalie, 4 years: "When we're writing we have to read and cross our legs".

Mind-mapping session, June

One child ventured, "You have to listen to the teacher – my daddy says so and you have to do what she says". Here the parent warns his son that he must comply with the life of the school.

As James and James argue,

> control is sometimes sought in order to prescribe some kinds of behaviours and to proscribe others, and not on the grounds of welfare but simply on the grounds of conformity ... a simple and yet very clear reflection of the process by which social order is maintained across and between generations. (James and James, 2004:3)

The quote encapsulates the authority of the parent over their child, and, more broadly, of adults over children as a social category. This child's story contributes to further understanding of how social relationships become inscribed with social meanings and how these get constructed and reconstructed over time (Bacon, 2012; Nicolopoulou and Richner, 2007). Notably, when the child in the above example explained that his daddy had said you had to listen to the teacher and do what she said, none of his peers raised an objection to this expression, underscoring a culture of conformity.

Gill, Winters and Friedman suggest that 'researchers have noted that parents' beliefs play an important role in shaping children's early experiences and that children are likely to learn those skills that are prized within a culture' (2006:215). Inevitably, from time to time children test out their potential to act in ways that go against what they have been 'taught or told to do' (James and James, 2004:4). However, just before the children were due to leave Lilybank, they were beginning to show signs of becoming more compliant and uncritical of school life and illustrated an expectation that 'the rules of democracy [may] not belong to them' (Bosio, 2012:144). Clearly, for the children a puzzling discrepancy existed between Lilybank and primary school.

Children shared their experiences with one another

Every morning in the early years setting, Mark ritually climbed up on the administrator's chair to wave to his mum and sister as they left the setting. Rory, Mark's friend, warned Mark that soon this was going to have to stop. Mark looked a little worried about this. Rory had an elder sibling at school, so he knew what to expect. "You won't be able to wave your mum off when you go to school. There are no windows. You have to say goodbye at the gate and you won't see her again until home time" (Rory to Mark, both 4 years, June).

This exchange from Rory to Mark yields insight into how children construct knowledge, how they plan, remember and solve problems between themselves, building on their own funds of knowledge and funds of identity. Funds of knowledge and funds of identity have great relevance here (e.g., in the ways that children exchange narratives). Esteban-Guitart and Moll (2013) explain:

> The term funds of identity refer to the historically accumulated, culturally developed and socially distributed resources that are essential for a person's self-definition, self-expression, and self-understanding. Funds of knowledge – bodies of knowledge and skills that are essential for the well-being of an entire household – become funds of identity when people actively use them to define themselves ... identity is made up of cultural factors such as sociodemographic conditions, social institutions, artifacts, significant others, practices, and activities. Consequently, understanding identity requires an understanding of the funds of practices, beliefs, knowledge, and ideas that [children] make use of. (Esteban-Guitart and Moll, 2014:31)

From the above example, we can understand how Rory's historically accumulated knowledge (i.e., his knowledge of school passed on from his elder sibling) is passed on to his friend. Furthermore, Rory has passed on his beliefs and knowledge of what will be expected in school. The beliefs and knowledge are what Esteban-Guitart and Moll (2014) define as funds of identity. Funds of knowledge and funds of identity can be useful concepts when considering children's narratives. In the following section parents share their child's stories; from this, we can see the value and importance of the funds of knowledge and funds of identity concepts as socially distributed stories are shared.

Parents shared their child's stories

> Froebel believed that educators should work closely with parents .... A child should feel a sense of harmony and continuity between [institution] and home, not a sharp division .... Ways to share information with parents can be found when there is a genuine desire and commitment to do so. (Tovey, 2017:121–122)

The EYPs at Lilybank believed they had a close relationship with most of their families, and perhaps due to this parents started to share their child's stories with the staff:

> When he realised that he would start school he told me "don't worry mummy I will be OK, you did your best to let me play at Lilybank and you will help me pick a good school". We will never know to what extent our own concerns about school influenced B's thinking, we tried to be calm and open about all our concerns without frightening him, trying to be positive about the next steps but it was a truly difficult balancing act as we were all facing the unknown (but some of us felt we knew a little of what was coming and did not like it one bit – me!!!). (Parent interview, October)
> We asked him about his feelings he said things like...

"I am curious about it".
"I wonder what I will learn".
"I know there will be rules, but I hope not too many".
"I think I will be made to sit still".
"I don't like staying still".
"I want to play, but I don't think I will be allowed to play there".
"I hope I find friends".
"If I don't like it, I hope I can stop".

He said he would have preferred to stay at Lilybank until he was 10 years old. He said he wanted to play and "that is what Lilybank does – lets me play". (Parent interview, October)

He was definitely exhausted by the end of each school day and sometimes cried saying, "I am just so tired" ... he would shout and bash things and when asked what was wrong he would sob ... and cry for a while .... He needed more physical connection than ever before, a need for quiet time ... he asked us not to go out in the evenings ... he did not want to join any clubs or extra activities. (Parent interview, October)

I asked him if he had any control over how his day unfolds each day at school. He said, "No I don't make the rules, only the teachers do". I explained that the teachers have told me they try to let the children choose as much as possible. He said, "I don't see that ... only older children get to decide at pupil parliament. I will have to be 8 or 9 before I get to decide anything". What would you like to decide upon ... he said "everything". (Parent interview, October)

[His] language changed within the first 2 months [of starting school]. He started talking about children as 'good' or 'bad'. He told me once he wasn't bad "because I do what the teacher says". (Parent interview, October)

One day [he] had a disagreement with a particular child in his class; they hit each other and were told by the teacher that this was not allowed and that they will now be punished for this behaviour and miss their playtime. The teacher said that during their play break they would be sent to another teacher [who had been trained in reconciliation]. The teacher was not able to see the children (busy) so they just had to follow their own teacher around for 20 mins while she tidied up the classroom. (Parent interview, October)

I have talked to many mums and dads about the first year, [name of parents], and all of the children's stories have variations but it seems to me that one thread runs through them all. School is hard work for children, it's tiring and frustrating at best and like a prison or army camp at worse. (Parent interview, October)

I don't know how much they are allowed to be different. They are made to conform. Slightly different to [Lilybank]. At school they rein them in a bit and if they are slightly different it could be an issue. (Parent interview, October)

We know [he] feels constrained and controlled at school so as soon as he is home we let him be, no rushing around, no unnecessary demands (he still has to operate as part of a family and be considerate to us and we to him) but as much as we can we keep it all calm and gentle. (Parent interview, October)

Equal dignity is not at the heart of the school policies. There is still a 'doing to' rather than a 'doing with' children. Teachers still see themselves as authority figures rather than 'partners in learning'. It is just good luck (or bad) who teaches the children, there are some very concerning behaviours from adults in the school, disrespectful dialogue (patronising children, even frightening children through lack of compassion or true desire to meet the child where they are) ... I feel the system isn't working fully for children no matter who the teacher is. (Parent interview, October)

The stories told from the child to the parent illustrated that there was no sense of celebrating who children were but only of who they were to become (Salmon et al., 2012). Levitas argues, above all we need to 'encourage in our children prophetic identities based on what they might become, rather than fixed [ascribed] identities' (Levitas, 2010:545). However, from the parents' stories, children were homogenised in the school environment, their stories buried.

Children's experiences of the school context

Once the children started school they shared the following:

"Too many rules, rules for everything".
"Not enough play".
"Play time should be longer".
"Teachers stop me playing before I have finished, they keep interrupting me playing with my friends".
"Why are all the doors locked? ... I don't feel free".
"I am not in charge of me anymore".

As a researcher in the school context, I too discovered the limitations the children experienced as illustrated in the following vignette:

> I was invited out into the playground today. I found myself to be very popular. Many children were keen to hold my hand and chat with me. There were other adults in the playground, pupil support assistants (known as PSAs). They did not engage with the children unless it was to give an order, i.e., stay on the paving stones, no pushing, no chasing etc. One supervisor did not vocalise her request, she simply looked at the child, pointed to a piece of litter and then indicated to the bin. The offending child was then expected to pick up the litter (dropped by him?) and put the dropped litter into the bin .... A girl I had never met before (perhaps from the other primary one class?) came up to me, laid her head on my thigh and said "I am going to be good today". (Field notes, August)
>
> Today it is raining ... when it came to morning break the teacher informed the children that due to the weather the children would not be going out today. Barry pushed his chair back, he enthusiastically ran from his seat and went out to the hallway ... he arrived moments later, he was smiling ... he was holding up his waterproof jacket ... he shouted to everyone "Don't worry you can go out if you have one of these". The teacher shouted, "Put that back and sit down!" Barry looked momentarily confused. He then put his head down, dragging his coat behind him he left the room to hang up his jacket. (Field notes, August)

Children were, on the whole, not encouraged to think for themselves or for their peers.

One of Froebel's essential principles was to acknowledge the child as a unique being: 'Each individual is unique, has the power to express himself in his distinctive way .... Each person, each child has a particular gift which will become visible if circumstances are right and freedom for expression is given .... Freedom, in Froebel's thinking, is a matter of education. It is the lack of opportunity, within the educational system, for children to make judgements and decisions which produces the adult's lack of ability to use freedom intelligently when he is given it' (Liebschner, 1992:36–37). However, I would argue, from my experience as a researcher, in school, this principle was largely unrealised.

Conclusion

This chapter has described children's narratives in relation to their experiences of educational transition. Children's stories about school, told directly to the researcher and to their parents, illuminate distinctions between what originally the children imagined school to be and their lived reality. This study has shown that not only are children's thoughts and experiences worth knowing about, but also that their narratives on the transition process are different from those of adults. For example, at some surprise to the parents, the children's stories presented a disjuncture of what was meaningful to them and what was important in the school context. These stories and commentaries from the children (and parents) reveal some of the ways power is exercised in the school environment. This study highlights the importance of listening to children's stories on the transition process

Special thanks are due to the children whose stories were analysed here.

Stomping giants and diamond castles

A study of the use of story grammars to support the development of coherence in written narrative within the context of a Froebelian play-based Primary 1 classroom

Catriona Gill

Introduction

From the moment of birth, we are storytellers. That first look or touch, the start of a lifelong journey of communication. Stories enable us to make sense of our lives, our thoughts, our ideas, our feelings and to pass on and share our history and culture. Storytelling is at the core of human existence, made possible by our extraordinary ability to develop and share complex systems of communication and meaning via the visual, textual, aural, linguistic and spatial languages we have developed. Our stories may be told through the languages of dance, painting, drawing, sculpture, film, theatre, books, music, spoken word and song. Marian Whitehead writes:

> A rich symbolic system such as that provided by language is necessary if children are to communicate and share in the life of a culture. (Whitehead, 2007:11)

Thus, when we are considering how we can help and support children to become better writers, it is essential that we continue to remind ourselves of the multimodal nature of human language and storytelling. And, as we move into the more formal stages of schooling, it is important that we do not narrow the curriculum into compartmentalised, mechanistic approaches.

> Writing and reading .... Lift man beyond every other known creature and bring him nearer to the realization of his destiny. Through the practice of these arts he attains personality .... The possession of the alphabet places the possibility of self-consciousness within his reach, for it alone renders true self-knowledge possible. (Froebel, 1826:224–225)

As education becomes more and more data driven and there is significant focused attention on closing socioeconomic attainment gaps, we run the risk of forgetting the importance of holistic approaches to developing language and storytelling. It is all too easy to focus on things that can be measured and packaged. As professionals, it is important to locate our practice in research, but we must also be cautious. Approaches and policy interventions based on findings from narrowly focused research studies can create situations in classrooms where the approaches become an end in themselves and we lose sight of the importance of rich language experiences. For example, the oft-quoted Hart and Risley (1995) study, which was one of the first to link vocabulary size to socioeconomic status, has resulted in a deficit perspective of language which not only reflects biases and stereotypes (Dudley-Marling and Lucas, 2009) but has also driven the development of narrowly focused programmes to 'boost' vocabulary. In the area of early reading instruction, Torgerson et al. (2018) found little evidence in a meta-analysis covering 452 separate studies to support one method of teaching phonics over another, and yet, the Department for Education and Skills (DfES) in England introduced systematic synthetic phonics as the defining aspect of early reading instruction (DfES, 2006) at the expense of a much more balanced approach, based mainly on the evidence of one study in Clackmananshire (Johnston and Watson, 2005).

At the time of this study, in my own classroom, I was expected to use an approach to writing which focused on vocabulary, connectives, openers and punctuation. Writing was to be improved by 'up levelling' sentences, essentially adding more or better vocabulary, connectives and so on. Assessment was based on children writing a letter – perhaps not the most appropriate genre for 5-year-olds who live in a time when messages are mostly sent via email and text and the majority of children are unlikely to have ever received a letter or seen one written.

This approach to teaching writing is focused on the technical aspects of writing separate from any understanding of what it means to be a writer. Froebel talks about the paucity of such approaches. If there is no context, no connection to the inner thought processes, no drive or impulse, no spark, then children are not interested or motivated to act.

> Nothing should ever be brought to the notice of the human being in purely arbitrary connection – in a connection that does not admit at least the possibility of discovering a necessary inner reason. The neglect of this makes instruction in writing, at present, so mechanical, lifeless, and dispiriting. (Froebel, 1826:224)

A central principle of a Froebelian education is the concept of making the inner outer and the outer inner, whereby children's life experiences are internalised and reflected upon and then are expressed through symbolic systems such as play, drawing, writing, modelling and the like.

Froebel felt that writing was an impulse that a child developed in response to a rich inner life, developed through the opportunity for experiences and thoughtful reflection. As the child accumulates experience and starts to become aware of it, 'he urgently feels the need to preserve his ideas and impressions in tangible form. So writing is developed' (Froebel, 1826, in Lilley, 1967:152).

Children need rich experiences provided by a developmentally appropriate early years curriculum which emphasises play, language and investigation in a context of adult support and guidance, for the urge to communicate in ways which preserve their ideas, in order to develop. They need to understand from within what it is to be a writer.

The purpose of play

> Play is the highest phase of child development .... It is highly serious and of deep significance .... The plays of childhood are the germinal leaves of all later life. (Froebel, 1826:54–55)

Play is a key aspect of Froebelian practice. It is recognised as a central integrating element in a child's development and learning. Its purpose, 'to guide children back upon their own nature' and 'to lead them onward to observe the life of the outer world' (Michaelis and Moore, 1891, in Lilley, 1967:24), is the essence of Froebel's understanding of the aim of education. This idea of play, as guiding children to understand the self and to grow towards understanding the world they are part of, is central to our humanity in the same way as is storytelling. As Gray (2008) writes, 'In play, from their own desires, children practice the art of being human'.

Vygotsky (1967) proposed that play, specifically sociodramatic or role-play, is the leading developmental activity of the child between the ages of 3 and 6, and rather than it being a free and spontaneous activity, without rules or social pressure, it is a way of exploring the world of social roles and relationships, where the motive is 'to act like an adult' (Elkonin, 1978, in Karpov, 2005:140).

Sociodramatic play, where children negotiate a play scenario, take on roles and develop a joint narrative, appears to have a key function in development and is characterised by symbolic representation and symbolic actions. There certainly appears to be support for the link between sociodramatic play and the development of symbolic representation. Dyachenko (1980, in Karpov, 2005:161) taught children how to use representational object substitutes such as sticks and paper cut-outs to support the retelling of a story and found that they could subsequently use their own substitutes to retell a new story, indicating that they had developed the ability to create a symbolic story model. In a similar way, it is quite likely that the use of symbolic objects during sociodramatic play also leads to the development of symbolic thought.

There is also a growing body of evidence (Bredekamp, 2004; Saifer, 2010) which suggests that play in the early years, specifically creative sociodramatic play (Smilansky, 1968), sensitively supported by early years practitioners, has an important impact on the development of executive functions, higher-order thinking and creativity. The key skills of working memory, inhibitory control, self-regulation and cognitive or mental flexibility are essential for future success at school and in life. That play is being shown to positively affect these skills strengthens the case for the centrality of play in an early childhood curriculum.

Play provides a courage all its own .... It provides not only a medium for exploration but also for invention. (Bruner, 1983)

Play, storytelling and narrative

Vivien Gussin Paley talks about play as 'story in action, just as storytelling is play put into narrative form' (1990:4), and Nicolopoulou (2016:8) sees young children's storytelling and sociodramatic play as 'complementary modes of their narrative activity, on a continuum ranging from the discursive exposition of narratives in storytelling to their enactment in pretend play'.

These narrative modes, discursive and enactive, initially emerge separately and distinctly. Children act out proto-narratives within their play even before they have command of spoken language. They focus first on character development and sets of actions, without much attention to narrative structure. As language develops and as they listen to the stories told around them, they start to tell their own stories, and in doing so, early narrative structures emerge. Although these narrative modes are initially distinct and complementary, Nicolopoulou (2016:23) suggests that 'pretend play and narrative should not be artificially separated and studied in mutual isolation. Instead, they should be viewed as closely related and often intertwined forms of socially situated symbolic action'. This is important, for when children have frequent opportunities to hear stories and tell stories and play out stories, these separate narrative modes start to converge and integrate, creating a 'powerful matrix for learning and development' (Nicolopoulou, 2016:24).

Given that a growing body of research (Feagans and Appelbaum, 1986; Pellegrini and Galda, 1993; Griffin, Hemphill, Camp and Wolf, 2004) shows that the mastery of narrative skills by children in their preschool years provides an important foundation for long-term literacy success, that between the ages of 3 and 6, narrative skills are a strong predictor of literacy skill at ages 8 to 10 (Wellman, Lewis, Freebairn, Avrich, Hansen and Stein, 2011), that children can learn skills that enable them to sustain and develop their sociodramatic play and that there are specific things that adults can do to support them (Smilansky, 1968), it seems essential that in our early years classrooms we offer an environment and pedagogical approach which supports the development and convergence of both enactive and discursive narrative and enables children to 'achieve effective narrative integration and cross-fertilization between pretend play and storytelling' (Nicolopoulou, 2016:16).

The storytelling and story acting approach developed by Vivian Gussin Paley (1990) and known more widely in the United Kingdom as helicopter stories (Lee, 2016) has been shown to have a positive impact on the development of narrative competence in young children (Nicolopoulou, Barbosa de Sa, Ilgaz and Brockmeyer, 2010; Nicolopoulou, 2016) as well as on the development of oral language skills, emergent literacy and social abilities. It appears to be the combination of storytelling and dramatisation that has the most powerful effect (McNamee, McLane, Cooper and Kerwin, 1985).

Much of the research has focused on oral storytelling, but when we turn to writing, the opportunity for enactive play also appears to have an important function in developing the quality of the discursive (written) narrative. Whitebread and Jameson (2010) found that children construct more creative and significantly better-structured stories when they have the opportunity to use props to act out and develop an already known story.

Narrative writing and the role of the adult

Thus, we can see that there is an important role for the adult in the classroom in providing a very particular environment and play-based pedagogy in developing children's narrative competence. A pedagogy based on play does not mean one where children are just left to get on with it on their own. It is crucial that educators 'observe, support and extend' (Bruce, 1987) and have an active, participatory role in their classrooms.

Froebel's concept of 'freedom with guidance', as explored by Liebschner (1992), stressed the important role of adults in supporting and guiding children. This is particularly important as they move from sensory experiences of the world towards expressing themselves symbolically, starting with play and moving to drawing and writing.

> To the child, the adult world of parent and teacher is important, for, without their support, he may be slow to start the ascent from the diversity of sensory experience to the unity of self-consciousness and, without their guidance, he may not be able to release his essential self or read the secret writing of the outer world. (Lilley, 1967:25)

If children are to become writers, it is also crucial that they have a wealth of experience from which to draw. Everyday things, such as going to the shops, playing in the park and helping at home, or less regular events such as family celebrations or visits to interesting or unusual places, opportunities to take part in a multitude of conversations and regular and frequent experiences of being read stories, gives children a foundation for their ideas and imagination.

Froebel wrote:

> Writing in pictures and in symbols assumes an over flowing richness of life in thought and experience. This richness gave rise to writing and only in virtue of it does the child develop a real need to write. Parents and teachers must, therefore, take care to make the life of their children's minds as rich as possible, not so much in diversity as in activity and meaning. (Froebel in Lilley, 1967:152)

It is especially important to consider how we can provide these rich experiences for children in our classrooms who may not have these types of opportunity at home. Children may spend long hours in school or childcare settings or after-school clubs when parents are working, and at the end of the day everyone is too tired for stories and conversations or going shopping together. It is also true that not all families are aware of the importance of these types of activities, and many feel they may not have the means to provide them.

A study of the use of story grammars to support the development of coherence in written narrative within the context of a Froebelian play-based Primary 1 classroom

This study took place within my Primary 1 class of 21 children, between the end of February and the end of June. In Scotland, children start Primary 1 in August between the ages of 4.5 and 5.5 years. The majority of children were at the time of the study between the ages of 5 and 6, and 40 per cent of them spoke English as an additional language (EAL). In addition, one child had complex additional support needs which included a diagnosis of autism spectrum disorder (ASD; this child had one-to-one support), another had been referred and was subsequently diagnosed with ASD and three children had a variety of other additional support needs. I had spent 2.5 years with most of the children, having taught them since they began nursery at the age of 3 years. A few children joined the class in August, at the beginning of Primary 1.

My practice is based on Froebelian principles, and my pedagogy reflects the Froebelian approach, with a significant focus on supporting high-quality, creative free-flow play. This was not straightforward in a Primary 1 classroom that was not well resourced for play, with a 1:20 adult:child ratio and the expectation that I deliver a synthetic phonics programme and a structured and mechanistic writing programme. However, I did what I could to provide a rich and imaginative curriculum with lots of hands-on experiences and opportunities for creative play whilst also meeting the expectations of senior management.

The curriculum I provided was literacy rich with a sustained focus on traditional tales and interactive storytelling. It was a multisensory approach which enabled the children to explore stories through puppets, small world, drama, block play, construction, drawing, painting, modelling and more. Traditional tales were specifically chosen because of the repetitive nature of the texts and their clear narrative structures. One traditional tale per term was explored at depth, and the children had the opportunity to develop characters within their play and embed the story structure through exploring the text in a variety of ways at story time and subsequently in their symbolic play. This particularly benefitted the children with EAL, as they had multiple opportunities to hear, internalise and reproduce the repetitive aspects of the text, and they also had the opportunity to use representational objects to create a symbolic story model (Dyachenko, 1980, in Karpov, 2005:161; Whitebread and Jameson, 2010).

I also drew on two approaches, *Foundations of Writing* (1986) and Pie Corbett's *Story Making* (now *Talk for Writing*; Corbett, 2008), to support the development of children's storytelling and writing.

Foundations of Writing was an approach developed from a project in several Scottish primary schools in the 1980s which sought an alternative way to teach writing from the previous 'copy it into your jotter' approach. Its overall aim was for pupils to be able to structure and compose writing independently for many purposes across the curriculum. Although it is now out of print, many early years teachers in Scotland still draw on this highly innovative approach in their teaching, in particular the use of expressive activities such as black line drawing, modelling, plasticine work and so on, to enable early story writers to communicate meaning to others. *Foundations of Writing* recognised that writing was often carried out as a solitary activity and early writers lacked the support provided by the social context within which speech takes place. Writing is also often separated from action, with a focus on the secretarial skills required rather than those of composition. In *Foundations of Writing*, writing becomes a group activity, connected to symbolic action and focusing on composition skills. Thus, it draws on the Vygotskian concept of the social nature of learning.

The *Foundations of Writing* drawing programme has two functions: to develop motor skills before children are taught the technical aspects of writing and to encourage children to tell stories in their drawings, which can then be scribed by an adult. Drawing resembles writing in a number of ways. The drawer has first to think about the subject and select what is to be drawn. A drawing can be modified and improved and can be made clearer by the addition of detail. By reminding children of experiences to draw (i.e., reaching up to switch off a light or reaching out to catch a ball), we support them to make a link with their own experiences. Using drama and mime, children can be supported to connect with how their body feels or how certain actions are carried out. Through offering these experiences, children's drawings, and subsequently their writing, improve significantly.

This was very evident in the work produced in my classroom. Quite quickly, the quality of the children's black line drawings improved significantly when ideas were discussed in a group and connected to action. In some of the writing that follows later in this chapter, this experiential process can be clearly identified in their writing.

The story-making approach aims to give children a bank of oral stories and narrative structures that they can draw on to inform their own writing. Children learn to tell a number of stories by heart using a pictorial or symbolic story map which is developed by the group. They use actions to support the storytelling, particularly for key connectives, and puppets, role-play and acting out are used to bring the story to life. This multisensory approach to understanding and sequencing narrative helps children to internalise narrative patterns which they can then refer to when innovating, by adapting well-known tales, or inventing, by creating new stories. There are certain similarities to the work of Dyachenko (1980, in Karpov, 2005:161), and the approach has also been shown to be a powerful strategy for improving the writing of boys and children with English as an additional language.

In my classroom, we initially focused on retelling The Little Red Hen. The children were highly engaged with the approach and were keen to create their own individual story maps to support their storytelling. Being able to tell a story from start to finish gave the children a feeling of control, and there was a positive impact on their confidence and self-esteem. The approach was particularly powerful for the children for whom English was an additional language as the opportunity to practise the story many times, supported by the actions and visual story map, helped them to learn the new language with confidence.

In addition to the above approaches, the group had some opportunities to explore the Vivian Gussin Paley story acting approach as developed by Trisha Lee (2016). However, this was not an embedded aspect of my classroom pedagogy.

Within this rich play-based literacy environment, the children were developing strong oral storytelling skills, and coherence within their spoken narratives was emerging; however, this was not translating to their written work, which was quite simplistic. Elements of character and setting were starting to develop in writing, but story structures, if present, tended to be very simple sequences with a lack of narrative cohesion.

So, the burning question was, how could I help the children to translate their oral ability into their written work?

Narrative coherence and story grammars

In order to construct a coherent story, children have to draw on their knowledge of narrative in order to develop the actions of their characters and to structure a sequence of events in a way that makes sense both temporally and causally. Shapiro and Hudson (1991) suggest that 'this may be accomplished by accessing schematic information that defines a set of rules governing the organization of categories and content of a story as defined by story grammar'.

Story grammars were first proposed by Rumelhart (1975) as a way of differentiating between 'the strings of sentences which form stories from strings which do not'. They provide an outline of the internal structure of the story. Stein and Glenn (1979:73) found that children recall stories in a highly organised way. Although they identified seven schemas or grammars in a simple story, they found that 'major settings, direct consequences and initiating events were the most frequently recalled'. It therefore made sense for me to focus on these key components with my early writers.

One of the strengths of using story grammar is that it supports children's understanding by explaining clearly the function of each grammar element. Using the terms *orientation* (or *characters and setting*), *problem* (or *dramatic event*), *resolution* (or *solving the problem*) rather than the much vaguer *beginning, middle* and *end*, which are so often used with young writers, gives children clear messages about how to structure a plot. Susan Dymock (2007:162) discusses the usefulness of story grammars in providing 'an overall structure for teaching narrative text structure awareness'. And Lewis (1999) suggests that explicitly teaching story structure and relating it to planning and mapping increases children's confidence and leads to increased coherence within their writing.

Case studies

Of the 21 children in the class, 11 formed the focus group. These children were selected because they had completed all four pieces of writing carried out during the study period. The focus group included several children with EAL, one with ASD and one with a strong history of dyslexia.

Four pieces of writing of different genres and structures were produced. The first and fourth writing samples were narrative stories and were analysed for cohesion and narrative structure.

Sample 1 was written at the end of February after a 6-week period exploring the story The Three Little Pigs. It was written before explicitly introducing the children to the concepts of story grammar.

Sample 4 was written at the beginning of June, following a 6-week period which initially started with the story Jack and the Beanstalk and subsequently developed into an exploration of giants and castles in response to the children's interests.

We used the story grammar elements (orientation, problem, resolution) to analyse stories we were reading in class and to help us structure our group story writing. The children developed their own characters through drama, role-play, modelling and character studies. We also had a class visit to a castle which gave the children an exciting and rich experience to draw on.

The following case studies look more closely at the work of four children from the focus group: Rose, Fergus, Laura and Emma.

Rose

Sample 1

The pig went to the farm
  Narrative element:

■ orientation

farm
fam

the   Pig wet
to the farm

Figure 11.1 Rose, sample 1.

Sample 4

Smartee pants eats grown ups and teachers. His teeth fall out. Go to the dentist and get false teeth

Narrative elements:

- orientation

- problem

- resolution

Fergus

Sample 1

The pig run away from the bad wolf.

Narrative element:

- resolution

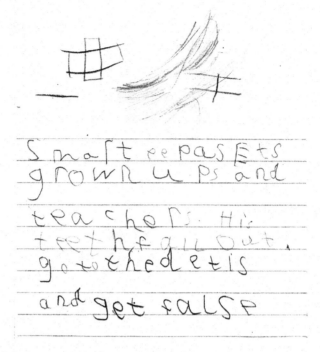

Figure 11.2 Rose, sample 4.

Figure 11.3 Fergus, sample 1.

Figure 11.4 Fergus, sample 4.

Sample 4

Once upon a time the lonely giant who was called Smiffe and has a rockpool, was paddling in the water. A big shark smelled him. He ate him. The end

Narrative elements:

- orientation
- problem
- resolution

Laura

Sample 1

my pig saw a muddy puddle It was a it was a muddy puddle and it saw a rain cloud the sun cames out there was a rainbow.

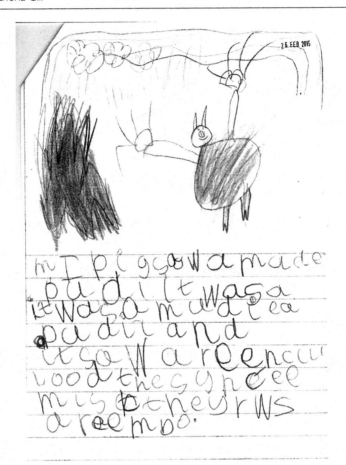

Figure 11.5 Laura, sample 1.

Narrative elements:

- orientation

- resolution

Sample 4

Once upon a time. In a castle there was a giant its name was Stompee. He liked his castle.

He has not got food. Anymore biscuits. He didn't have any money.

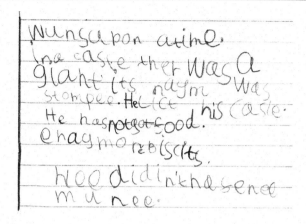

Figure 11.6 Laura, sample 4.

But he went to work for a few days then he got money and bought food again and he lived happily ever after. The end

Narrative elements:

- orientation

- problem

- resolution

Emma

The 3 little pig's went to the shops and then the big bad wolf came in the shops looking for the 3 pig's. the pig's were scared and the pigs got eaten by the big bad wolf

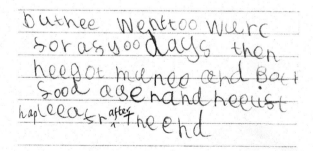

Figure 11.7 Emma, sample 1.

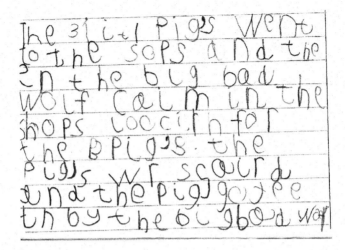

Figure 11.8 Emma, sample 4.

Figure 11.9 Analysis of writing, sample 1.

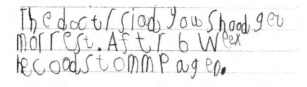

Figure 11.10 Analysis of writing, sample 4.

Narrative elements:

- orientation
- problem
- resolution

Once upon a time there was a giant called Stommpy. Stommpy lived in a castle that was made out of diamonds. When he stomped, his feet got louder and louder. One day he couldn't stomp any more. He called the doctor the doctor rushed over. The doctor said you should get more rest. After 6 weeks he could stomp again.

Narrative elements:

- orientation
- problem
- resolution

Analysis

On analysis of the work of the 11 children in the focus group, it was clear that the writing in The Three Little Pigs stories (Sample 1) was very simple and had little structure. More than half of the children incorporated only one story grammar element, and only three pieces of writing contained all three story grammar elements of orientation, problem and resolution.

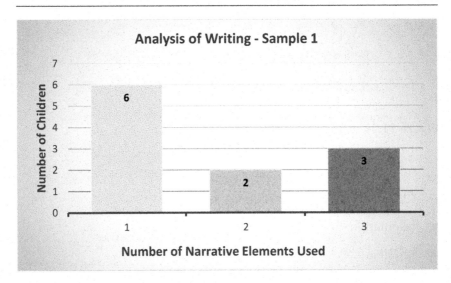

Figure 11.11

However, analysis of the giant stories clearly shows a significant improvement in narrative coherence. All 11 children were able to use two or three narrative elements in their stories, and nine included all three narrative elements. The three children whose first piece of writing had included three elements produced writing that was much more clearly structured and detailed.

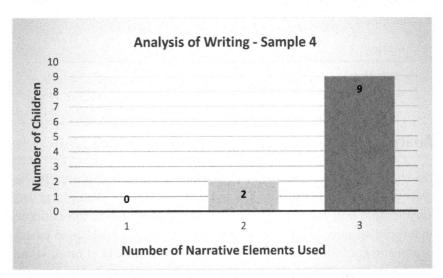

Figure 11.12

Conclusion

Although limited conclusions can be drawn from this small-scale enquiry, it is clear that providing a rich, creative, multisensory environment and a pedagogy which supports symbolic play enables both enactive and discursive narrative modes to develop and begin to intertwine. Adult guidance through the use of story grammars further brings these narrative modes together and has a positive impact on the development of narrative structure and coherence in children's writing.

Key messages

Rich, holistic approaches are important in developing language and storytelling, particularly for children with EAL and communication or language difficulties. Sociodramatic play appears to have a key function in development and is characterised by symbolic representation and symbolic actions.

Storytelling and sociodramatic play are complementary modes of narrative activity and initially emerge separately and distinctly. An environment and pedagogical approach which supports the development and convergence of both enactive and discursive narrative enables children to achieve integration of these narrative modes. Writing is an impulse that children develop in response to a rich inner life that is developed through the opportunity for experiences and thoughtful reflection.

Using story grammars to explicitly teach narrative structures supports children to develop narrative coherence in their story writing.

Gathering thoughts about storytelling

Tina Bruce

Before we do anything else, as we arrive at the end of this book, we need to bring together the work that has been undertaken by the authors in order to gather together our thoughts and establish, with as much clarity as possible, what storytelling is. In the first chapter, Jane Whinnett introduced us to the authors and their chapters, which is a story in itself.

What has emerged is that although throughout the book we use the term *story*, it is not as easy to define or categorise as other forms, such as a poem or a drama. Northrop Frye (1957, in Haven, 2007:19) suggests that 'we have no word for a work of prose other than *story*'. We describe a huge range including tale, fable, myth, legend, fairy tale, folk tale, parable and epic. Because we have no working definition of what a story is, Haven (2007:20) suggests that we should look at how our minds process, understand, create meaning and remember incoming narrative information. This is difficult to do, because we are only just at the beginning of understanding how human brains work. What is clear is that stories seem to have been part of being a human since the beginning of humanity. The fields of evolutionary biology and neuroscience can give some clues. These clues are found in cave paintings and rock pictures. People still sit together around a fire or share food and tell stories. Stories work well in the dark, at bedtime, before we go to sleep. Other ways of building our understanding of the hugely important contribution stories make to our humanity come from our ponderings, explorations and reflections about culture and identity. *Reflecting Realities: Survey of Ethnic Representation within UK Children's Literature 2018*, undertaken by the Centre for Literacy in Primary Education (CLPE, 2019), suggests that books published in the United Kingdom need to pay more attention to culture and diversity.

The value of reflecting realities, individuals, identities, cultures and communities is rooted in the importance of elevating all lived experiences and recognising them as worthy of note and exploration. To understand and to be understood is at the heart of human experience. (CLPE, 2019:4)

Charmian Kenner (2000) and book companies such as Letterbox have always emphasised the importance of the cultural aspects of literacy learning. This begins with communication, language and stories.

How children develop an understanding of story formation, structures and its architecture is another fascinating strand.

A story involves us in the different ways in which our minds deal with information that we process through the mechanism of narrative and

identifies the specific informational elements that trigger the creation of meaning, that enhance meaning, and that form the central structure of stories. (Haven, 2007:6)

It seems to be easier for human beings (children and adults alike) to make meaning and to understand and use narrative information which comes in a structured story form. Haven (2007:27) even argues that through evolution the brain 'has engineered story pathways as express routes into the human mind'. We see this in the way that religions across the world, both mainstream and less so, since the beginning of time, have used and continue to use stories to explain, help people to understand and make meaning. There are also what Marian Whitehead (2004) suggests 'community narratives', which are specific to a group who together experience things that those outside the group do not. This can be anything from a communal outing to the sea to a family celebration of a birth to something that is specific to that group or tribe, village, club or school. Children who, from an early age, enjoy listening to stories are better able to 'process, absorb, and remember the incoming information' (Haven, 2007:7).

We also know that children, as part of this, develop a sense of belonging with stories they enjoy and return to again and again. Denny Taylor (1983:87) suggests that children remember these stories with affection for the rest of their lives. Colin Harrison (1996:25) suggests that family times with stories (and literacy as a whole) are important for children to experience. He suggests that storytelling situations often arise spontaneously. When intergenerational happenings develop, they enrich stories. His point is an important one, because when parents, grandparents, carers, older siblings and family friends gather for a story to be created, read or told, an atmosphere of belonging, feeling safe, deep concentration and focus emerges. This is powerful in developing learning.

Literacy tends to be seen as learning to read and write. The part played by storytelling is not always given the central place it should have, either in family life or in educational settings. Stories do something which, if left out, slow down the progress into an enjoyment of reading (both literature and non-fiction) and writing (both facts and fiction). For this reason, Margaret Meek (1985:43) stresses the need to 'foreground the emotive'. She sees emotion as an integrating force in children's experiences. As well as listening to stories and taking part in making stories, as well as interacting with text when sharing a storybook with an adult, children spontaneously produce nonsense rhymes and jokes that are a very important aspect of their being active in their language development.

Most of the literature on storytelling and the development of literacy focuses on children who are becoming spoken/sign language users, typically from the age of 2 onwards. But children begin to understand what a story is long before this kind of development emerges. This was realised by Friedrich Froebel (1782–1852), who wrote what he felt to be his most important work in 1844. He created the Mother Songs, which we now call the Family Songs, in recognition of the importance of introducing babies to stories in ways which speak to them and engage their fascination (Bruce, 1987; Bruce and Spratt, 2008; Bruce, 2019:86, 110, 370). The Family Songs (including the finger plays and action songs on the spot) enhance the developing symbolic understandings of the baby/toddler through the forms of beauty, everyday life experiences and knowledge. The baby sees the whole clenched hands of the adult held up and these become the apples growing on the tree, which as it sways in the wind sheds the apples, which are gathered in a basket made by weaving the fingers together from both hands. Froebel introduces the baby to the way a real experience of seeing real apples growing on a tree, put in a basket and eaten, can be represented symbolically through finger plays and whole-body movements. The emotive, emphasised by Meek, is foregrounded as the baby sits on the loved and loving adult's knee. Gradually the link with moral development and encouragement of self-discipline becomes embedded, without words, into this play episode.

There is an ethos in which the person who gathers the apples for the family to eat has worked hard and is valued and appreciated. But the moral aspect is not preached. Neither is the need for self-discipline in doing the gathering so that the family can share the food. But both elements are gently there in the pictures accompanying the Family Songs. As Fabetti (2005) demonstrates, what is not there is as important as what is there. From the beginning what is good and what is evil is, in a nuanced way, being explored. This is the stuff of drama, the juxtaposing of good versus evil so evident in Greek and Shakespearian plays, presented in an appropriately subtle way.

Work over many years by Colwyn Trevarthen (1993) shows how babies communicate and 'speak' to those close to them in non-verbal ways. They move in synchrony with the voice of the parent or sibling in a dance-like fashion. They 'reply' when spoken to if their conversation partner pauses long enough for them to reply instead of constantly 'talking at' the baby. Trevarthen's (1998) ongoing work with a group of musicians (Malloch and Trevarthen, 2009) demonstrates that in these proto-conversations babies understand beginnings, middles and endings, as they will complete a musical phrase to round off a joint episode. They have a sense of the whole, and they work with this understanding before they can make a story in words or signs.

The late Vivian Gussin Paley's pioneering work has influenced the authors in this book. She wrote the foreword for a book edited by Cremin, Flewitt, Mardell and Swann:

> The narrative begins in the baby's crib and may well be the earliest design for storytelling …. 'Peek-a-boo' sounds like the original lost and found plot, acted out of the fear of being left alone. What a joy to act out these dramas again and again as the child grows older and happily, a vehicle has been provided free of charge. It is play and its natural counterpart, storytelling, just a step away from play and recognisable by every child. (Gussin Paley in Cremin, Flewitt, Mardell and Swann, 2016:vii)

Guy Dartnell and Tom Morris developed, commissioned by *Crying Out Loud* (Gladstone, 2004), 'Oogly Boogly' for very young children, not yet speaking, and their grown-ups. Each session is for eight babies at a time (12–18 months) with four performers. The experience takes place inside a safe, inflated structure designed by Architects of the Air, where the performers follow the children's every sound, move and mood to discover a new meeting place between the worlds of baby and adult. It is improvisatory and utterly unpredictable for everybody involved. No words are spoken. The communications are entirely non-verbal and without sign language. It works with babies on the edge of language and young children with autism who do not yet speak. Children begin to make stories. One child began to crawl to the other side of the room, and a performer moved in parallel with him. The baby continued. At the other side, another performer joined him and the three of them went to the other side. The baby laughed and led the group across to the other side, enjoying the feeling of being in control and joined by the next performer. And so the story unfolded.

Non-verbal communication that is supported develops into multi-layered and sophisticated communication and storytelling surprisingly early in babies and toddlers. Robert Fabetti (2005), speaking at a Leaparts conference, said:

> Listening is complex. It means paying attention to what is not said, to the hidden, the evoked ... the act of listening and paying attention to what happens creates an environment of complicity, where it is possible to tell the visible as well as the non-visible, the hidden, the concealed, the mysterious. (Fabetti, 2005)

In the theatre performance for children who were on the edge of spoken/signed language, children saw adults create huge clay structures and mounds of wet sand with dry sand cascades and pour water from a huge jug to a massive cauldron. They were deep in concentration and fully engaged throughout. They felt the story as different characters appeared and used the materials. At the end they were invited to come to the stage to use all the materials – water, clay, sand – that had been part of the 'story'.

Examples of storytelling for toddlers who are speaking/signing can be found at the Angel Theatre in Islington, London, where puppets are often used, and the Polka Theatre in Wimbledon in London, which has undertaken a project with a Sure Start children's centre/maintained nursery school under the guidance of Jo Belloli.

Babies and toddlers who have the kind of experiences outlined by Trevarthen, Malloch, Dartnell, Morris, Fabetti and Belloli are learning about the structuring of stories. This becomes a resource as they move deeper and deeper into the journey of literacy.

Research, for example the longitudinal and cross-cultural study by Rathnarsdottir (2006), demonstrates how children who have experienced rich pretend play in their early childhood years engage more readily and easily with more complex and sophisticated levels of both reading comprehension and creative writing, which blossoms and burgeons with strength from about 9 years of age. Because the children have engaged from 3 to 7 years in rich pretend play, they are familiar and comfortable with ideas such as before this happens that happens, and after, this will take place. They have mastered the logic and structure of making complex stories. First, they achieve this in the play scenarios they create, and later it takes form in creative writing and reading with meaning.

Further evidence for the importance of play in its contribution to helping children learn to find form and structure in listening to and telling stories is found in the research of Milda Bredikyte and Pentti Hakkarainen (2017), who have examined how mature narrative play develops. Milda Bredikyte teases out the tension between adults directing play when they join it and the power of sharing play with children. On the one hand,

> play is the first independent activity of which the child keeps control. Play is the space where children are able to practise their ideas and all possible skills in an independent manner. In other situations, young children are guided by the adult and have to accept adult imposed rules and themes. In a way, adults are constantly 'dragging' children to their developmental level in this way underestimating the most important and the most interesting period of their development. (Bredikyte, 2017:4)

This chimes with both the Vygotskian (1978) and the Froebelian approach to education (Bruce, 2017:9; 2019). As play matures, it opens up the opportunities and creates the mechanism for transformation into well-structured writing and reading and later workplace attitudes which employers find useful and seek. The pleasure of childhood pretend play alongside Froebel's gifts, occupations, movement and arts of music, dance and engagement with nature come together, providing fulfilment in work and life as a whole. It is important to emphasise the role of a rich, broad and deep curriculum framework. In this book, stories and how they are listened to and told by adults and children are valued in a variety of forms. These include pretend play, drawings and paintings, in nature contexts, in picture books and in books with texts. An important study by the Centre for Literacy in Primary Education (CLPE, 2019) using randomised control research methods demonstrates the power of using picture books with children in primary schools from 5 to 11 years. This is an especially helpful way of introducing stories to children who are learning English as an additional language, for children with special educational needs and disabilities as well as being very fruitful for all children in the schools. At first the children (especially those who were from 9 to 11 years old) thought these books were babyish, but as they explored the depth, nuances and layerings they came to understand the sophistication that was present.

What might appear to be babyish to children in middle childhood in Western cultural contexts may be a feature of an era in which children are expected to accelerate through childhood and be adult as soon as possible. It is difficult to see any advantage in speeding up and going against biology. Just as the CLPE is finding that older children benefit from picture stories, so in an earlier time Froebel found that older siblings enjoyed performing finger plays with the babies and toddlers in their family. And Froebel created these so that the stories were nuanced and sophisticated. The finger plays and action songs draw the attention of older children and adults to the importance of the relationship between self-awareness and location of self in relationship with others and the community, a relationship that goes beyond the known to communities never met, connection with nature and the enormity of the universe. This Froebelian framework chimes with stories, often through poetry, offered to the youngest children which are written by deeply appreciated writers. Michael Rosen's CLIPPA award-winning anthology (2015) *A Great Big Cuddle* is an example.

It is not unusual in some Western cultural contexts to find children from 5 to 7 years beginning to feel they ought not to indulge in pretend play as that might seem babyish. There is a problem in discouraging and cutting off pretend play as part of education from the age of 4 or 5 years. Evidence is gathering that pretend play, if encouraged and made strong through experience and support, matures by the age of about 7 years, and the transformation into well-structured and formed story writing and good comprehensible reading for pleasure and purpose will be constrained without it. In a school using a Froebelian approach, 8-year-olds in the year 3 class in England, or Primary 4 in Scotland, are traditionally known as being in transition.

There is an irony in the fact that there is nothing babyish about babies. As Alison Gopnik (Gopnik, Meltzoff and Kuhl, 1999) points out, even in the first few months babies evaluate, observe and imitate. It is therefore important to build on these strengths and to support and actively provide ways of deepening them. Froebel felt that the Mother Songs (which were really family songs) that he developed as his last work (1844) were his most important. The work of Colwyn Trevarthen across the years, looking at the ways babies respond to songs with stories in them, sends a strong message: stories predate language!

Babies anticipate the words, join in movement with sad and happy themes, finish tunes and bring completion. It goes without saying that babies, and even young children, are not yet able to grasp and engage with the social problems and issues which often enter the stories appreciated by older children and adults. However, Betty Bacon (in Meek, Warlow and Barton, 1977:129) suggests that from the beginning realism means 'truth to feeling'. This is what makes a good story for a child. For this reason, Elaine Moss (in Meek, Warlow and Barton, 1977:129) writes that she came to understand why a little girl called Alison loved a story about a peppermint pig, which was not, in her adult view, great literature. She loved it because she, like the pig, was adopted. Stories help us to make meaning of our lives.

A baby who is bounced up and down on the adult's knee while sung to is learning that in this story they will have an adventure of being lifted high but will return safely to sit on the knee. Babies delight in the repetition, the anticipation of this, predicting what comes next in the story. But they only enjoy this if the adult is someone they know and trust and who is sensitive to their responses and signals. Then they enjoy their predictions being confirmed, or show surprise at something different from the expected, so that form and structure is played with. Babies demand completion. Trevarthen developed our understanding of proto-conversations in babies prior to their developing spoken/signed language. In Froebel's Mother (Family) Songs, we see proto-stories in the process of development.

Stories are biologically as well as culturally and socially driven. They allow us to escape from the constraints of real life. They help us to consider what might be (which helps provide us with ways to change what is and to predict what might be in the future). This gives a feeling of control and well-being. James Britton writes:

> Storying is the most significant way we explain how we came to be where we are, and a universal language habit that transcends all cultural barriers. We are cut off from its origins by the device of writing. (Britton, 1970, in Meek, Warlow and Barton, 1977:8)

He goes on to say that the stories we come to love as adults are 'developed and refined from earlier forms and response to stories at each stage of growth'. Stories are a basic way of organising human experience, according to Barbara Hardy (1968, in Meek, Warlow and Barton, 1974:12). In her view, great stories, those that adults return to again and again, combine the personal and the impersonal. But, of course, for babies and little children the personal is central. She suggests that we delude ourselves if we think that we begin with fairy tales during childhood and tell truths in later adulthood. In reality, she says, we oscillate between fairy tales and what is true.

Continuing with this theme, of the tension between what is real and what is imagined, James Britton (1970, in Meek, Warlow and Barton, 1974:40–41) sees using language to tell stories as a powerful way to show ourselves both the actual world and also unreal and imagined worlds. He suggests that when we put our experiences into words, we order them in a particular way and that this is an important process. It means that we can, through stories, lessen the intensity of our real experiences and our imagined fears. As the work of Vivian Gussin Paley, Dowley McNamee, Bredikyte and Hakkarainen, Athey, Bruce, Gura and Applebee shows us, although young children are on the journey of developing and putting stories into words, they find it challenging to articulate them. They can do this more readily through pretend play and other forms such as in wooden block play, model making, drawing and other occupations (clay, drawing, woodwork, cooking, painting, weaving, sewing, stick-laying, parquetry, construction and more). In their play, children tell stories.

When children engage in pretend play, they improvise freely and bring in events and experiences they encounter in the real world. This equips and strengthens them to return to the real world and meet the demands and challenges there. Winnicott (1947) describes this as a 'harmonious relationship between inner needs and external demands'. There is, he argues, a cultural pool of humanity

> into which individuals and groups of people may contribute, and from which we may all draw if we have somewhere to put what we find. (Winnicott in Meek, Warlow and Barton, 1977:47)

That is a function of stories. They give us, Winnicott suggests, somewhere to put what we find. For young children, stories are put into pretend play and related material. Stories seem to fit into our bank of previous experiences (Bruner, 2003). They chime with the way things happen. He also argues (1990) that stories might at times deviate from our experiences, which gives them a sense of excitement and adventure. Supposing this, or what if that ...

According to Haven (2007), in stories, experience builds on expectation. But a story must make sense. (We are back to Betty Bacon's 'truth to feeling' again.) A story, Haven says, needs to have meaning and characters who have goals and intentions but whose efforts play an important part in the conflicts and struggles they face.

> When we listen to a melody we do not consider individual notes as isolated elements. Rather, each note is understood as part of a sequence as a whole. Each note takes on meaning only in relation to the note that has preceded it and in anticipation of that which will succeed it. Human minds do the same thing with narrative. But instead of using melody to impose meaning, we use mental story templates (maps). Individual experiences only assume meaning within the context of a time-based, sequenced story. (Haven, 2007:35)

Recent forms of story may not be so sequenced in a linear form with the arrival of postmodernism and other genres, but as the work of Rathnarsdottir (2006) shows, children who have engaged in pretend play are equipped to explore different ways and structures and forms in the telling of stories. The key message here is that, as Froebel (Bruce, 2019:123–124) emphasised, stories are part of the way in which children begin to make the inner outer and the outer inner. These can be spoken or created by other means. At the Sixth Early Childhood Convention in New Zealand, Arapera Royal Tangaere (1995), in giving the challenge to delegates, said:

> I always draw on my two cultures as beacons to guide me. To my Maori world, I always face the past: that which is known for the wisdom of my ancestors, and move backwards into the future. To my Pakeha world, I always face the future with excitement and trepidation. For me I have to face both ways .... My challenge to early childhood education is to look both within ourselves and draw upon the strength that each of us have and look outside ourselves, so that we can see our direction. (In Bruce, 2005)

Some cultures, such as the Maori, are traditionally oral storytellers. Other cultures have lost this and are more constrained. When the oral tradition is strong, story making and storytelling have a powerful and central place in helping both children and adults to locate, dwell in and integrate their inner and outer worlds. The Nordic cross-cultural longitudinal study undertaken by Rathnarsdottir (2006) demonstrates that making the inner outer and the outer inner (Froebel in Bruce, 2019:123–124) equips children so that later on they can tell complex stories and write them down. This is often called creative writing. Frank Kermode (1969) suggests that

> when we invent fictions in dreams and make-believe we meet ourselves in them and the end is delayed. When we tell stories for others, we draw to a close, a pay-off time, and part of the pleasure is the form as the box-lid snaps shut. When we read a story we both experience events as we read (in Harding's and Britton's 'spectator role') and we also remember the story as a story when we have read it. As a memory it is what Aristotle calls a 'completed action'

to be contemplated in a way that life cannot be. (Kermode, 1969, in Meek, Warlow and Barton, 1977:73–74)

This is important, because it means that the stories we tell (or read) to children connect them to the inherited culture of their community and gradually larger society. They inherit phrases such as 'Once upon a time' and 'They all lived happily ever after'. Kermode (1969:73–74) suggests that in this way they begin to see how a story that has been written down and read to them uses conventions with its own rules, and they learn to use these in the stories they create and gradually write down and read to others. This means that the inner world of the child is, Kermode believes, 'wrested' from the writer as it is shaped into a story. Meek, Warlow and Barton (1977:74–75) suggest that the writer then offers to the audience what Tolkien calls a 'secondary world' and what Winnicott calls the 'third area' in which 'literary belief' gives opportunities to make a story that is not real in life. This process deepens such that gradually, as children read more literature and are told more stories, they are in a position to encounter stories where the authors vary the inherited patterns of story more and more. However, during early and into middle childhood, children 'while they are young and becoming acquainted with story, make considerable imaginative investments in coherent patterns' (Meek, Warlow and Barton, 1977:75).

Part of building up the possibility of being able to deviate from the inherited patterns of story making and then storytelling/writing lies in the way children cry out for a story to be repeated again and again. C. S. Lewis (1969:87) 'sees unexpectedness as central to a good story'. He suggests that 'children understand this well when they ask for the same story over and over again and in the same words'. Children are storing up their bank of inherited phrases to use in their stories. Folk tales and fairy stories give children a resource of these, and they become what C. S. Lewis calls 'a rich canon of words'. Michael Rosen's *We're Going on a Bear Hunt* has, as an example, entered this canon of literature as a more modern story alongside the traditional Three Little Pigs and other folk and fairy tales.

James Britton (in Meek, Warlow and Barton, 1977:107) argues that we should aim to 'refine and develop responses the children are already making to fairy stories, folk songs, pop songs, television serials, their own game-rhymes and so on. Development can best be described as an increasing sense of form'. However, Britton is in good company with writers such as C. S. Lewis and Michael Rosen in cautioning adults to be aware that this sense of form needs to grow from within the child.

> It is the legacy of past satisfactions. It may become articulate, find-ing expression in comment and criticism, but equally it may not. (Britton in Meek, Warlow and Barton, 1977:108)

When children do enter into lively discussions about a story told to them, they tend to talk about the characters and the narrative. Certainly, I have never heard a child respond to a story they have engaged with by saying how much they liked the way it was structured, the techniques, devices or form. Britton (1978: 108) is clear that 'we should be more afraid of introducing such matters too early than too late'.

If this applies to stories we tell and read to children, it is even more so when they read us or tell us stories they create. As Britton (1978: 108) points out, the poet Robert Frost said, 'You cannot worry a poem into existence, though you may work upon it once it is in being'. When children first begin to create stories in writing, they may not yet be open to having them 'corrected' into tightly conventional forms. The main thing is to flow with characters and narratives and the use of real life as a powerful resource to draw upon. The pioneering work of the late Vivian Gussin Paley has been referred to and used to good effect by authors in this book. Because children are able to tell their stories, and see the adult write them down with their dictation, and then have the opportunity to see them acted out, they have the possibility to take control and 'work upon it once it is in being'. They usually sort this out themselves, and it shows in their subsequent stories rather than at the time the story is acted out.

Vivian Gussin Paley's approach gives children what they need for their early storytelling/writing. Her work chimes with the Froebelian way of working through, in which children develop a sense of the Froebelian forms of beauty and everyday life and some understanding in place of the knowledge of what makes a story come into being, which can be shared by telling or writing for others to hear or read. Kendell Haven (2007:ix) argues that understanding 'story architecture' comes relatively easily for young children because it is deeply human. This makes the later devel-opment into reading and writing stories more manageable. In the history of humanity, oral storytelling dominated. Stories are still passed down orally in some cultures where this has not been lost.

> Every culture in the history of this planet has created stories: myths, fables, legends, folk tales. Not all have developed codified laws. Not all have created logical argument. Not all have created written language and exposition. All developed and used stories. (Haven, 2007:4)

Earlier in the chapter there was some reference to the need for children to build both good and evil into their understanding of stories. Catherine Storr is very clear that

> where there is a story, there must be a conflict, and where there is a conflict there must be Good and Evil, in however watered down a version. (Storr in Meek, Warlow and Barton, 1977:123)

She goes on to argue that

> evil is within as well as without, and by understanding your own feelings we have the power over evil in others that understanding gives. (p. 126)

Froebel believed that education leads to children and adults becoming aware of themselves in all their relations and that self-awareness is a deeply important part of this. Only with self-awareness can we have a sense of others. And this is needed if there is to be a sense of audience in telling a story. A story is a shared experience, as is the way it is formed into a shape that can be shared.

In dealing with evil, it is important to note that fairy tales present violence, fear and evil in a remote context. The distancing is important and contrasts with stories presenting violence in a real way that might be part of a child's real life. This can be overwhelming, because it is too close to reality. Milda Bredikyte and Pentti Hakkarainen (Bruce, Hakkarainen and Bredikyte, 2017; Bredikyte, 2017) have explored this in their work on what constitutes mature narrative play.

> Zaporozhets (1986) compares the structure of a fairy tale and play. He saw the difference between them in terms of abstractness. A fairy

tale requires imagining the whole story: the event, physical environment, persons, their relations, emotional states etc. But in pretend
play peers and the use of concrete props and tools may support story
construction .... Story and play are often so closely connected that
they are often inseparable. (Bredikyte, 2017:41)

There can be stories which are about unhappy situations, but these need
to be redemptive in some way so that problems and challenges encoun-
tered during the story are dealt with. Redemption and some kind of
resolution need to be present. Susan Isaacs (1930) believed that in their
play children can escape from evil if they find they are losing a feeling
of being in control. It is possible to escape from the play scenario. But
when we tell stories which might be frightening to children, they cannot
have the same control as they do when they play, so we need to bear this
in mind and be sensitive to children's feelings and responses. It is useful
to bear in mind that, as Haven (2007:128) states, 'fiction is a process of
mental construction that produces "human truth"'. Haven then quotes
Freeman (2003): 'The only meaningful difference between fiction and
non-fiction is that fiction describes events that haven't happened yet'.
  Haven (2007) illustrates this giving an example from Gordon Mills
(1976). If, as adults, we know the story of Hamlet, then a visit to a castle
is influenced by the story.

Suddenly the walls and ramparts speak a different language. The
courtyard becomes an entire world, a dark corner reminds us of
the darkness of the human soul. (Mills, 1976, in Haven, 2007:9)

An example from children would be that Lila (3 years, 6 months) loves
ballet and has watched on her grandmother's mobile phone parts of
the Bournonville ballet dancing La Sylphide. Her grandmother makes a
Sylphide dress out of net curtains for Lila and her sister Stevie (5 years,
6 months). For several weeks they dance to the music, but Lila keeps
asking for the story to be repeated and she keeps wanting to watch
extracts on the phone. On a visit to the New Forest they go with their
grandmother and father into a glade and act out the story, improvising
both the dancing and the telling of the story as they go.
  Haven (2007:15) emphasises that stories are about the way information is structured rather than just a means of conveying information.

That is why the story engages the audience who receive it and respond to it. Haven argues that four things matter in a story. Those listening must find themselves paying attention, making meaning, remembering and recalling the story. Stories enhance memory, so recalling becomes easier. Mandler and Johnson (1984 and 1977, in Haven) found that stories (and the information in them) are remembered better and longer than the same information when it is simply given as a set of information.

In this book about storytelling we have focussed on babies, toddlers and young children at the beginning of their journey into becoming story makers and storytellers and writers. The early finger plays and family songs pioneered by Froebel remain important and chime with current research. Pretend play is a powerful mechanism engaging children to travel further and with commitment and engagement deeper into this process. Through their pretend play, children grapple with the establishment of characters and the architecture of the plot and narrative so that their stories develop in shape and form. Mature play (Bruce, Hakkarainen and Bredikyte, 2017; Bredikyte, 2017) leads to more sophisticated and deeper levels of storytelling from children.

As they enter the school system, the storytelling (providing it is not squashed by an overemphasis on the mechanics of writing as part of the schooling institutions and government controls) ripens in middle childhood so that by about 9 years of age children are able to read sophisticated literature. However, Cremin, Flewitt, Mardell and Swann (2016) point out that

> nonetheless in accountability cultures, where early years educators are pressurised by the 'drive to literacy' and policy expectations regarding contested concepts such as 'reading readiness' (Whitebread and Bingham, 2012), practitioners often find it hard to make space for children's stories. (Cremin, Flewitt, Mardell and Swann, 2016: 23)

'Reading for pleasure is more important to a child's educational achievement than their family's wealth or social class' (OECD, 2002). They have the possibility of becoming creative writers of stories because they are experienced in the mechanics and structuring of the architecture of story form. This will depend on training practitioners and teachers

(Bruce, 2019:349–367) to embrace the essentials of storytelling, giving children rich educationally worthwhile experiences, orally telling stories, with and without props, reading stories to children, making stories with them, acting them out, encouraging and empowering mature and sophisticated play to develop, helping children to wallow in a rich and diverse canon of literature with plenty of rhyme and inherited phrases as part of this, so that children bring all these resources into their storytelling, reading and writing. Pascal, Bertram and Rouse (2019) reviewed a wealth of literature supporting this approach, along with the evidence gathered together by Cremin, Flewitt, Mardell and Swann.

Working together as a community of practice in developing this book about storytelling has felt reaffirming. Storytelling matters. It leads to a situation such that children live in ways which appreciate the creativity of others but are also able to be creative themselves. This is one of the main contributors towards well-being and a sense of fulfilment (both for the children and those who spend time with them).

References

Alderson, A. (2008) *Young Children's Rights – Exploring Beliefs, Principles and Practice*. 2nd Edition. London: Jessica Kingsley.

Aliakbari, M. and Faraji, E. (2011) *Basic Principles of Critical Pedagogy*. Paper presented at the 2nd International Conference on Humanities, Historical and Social Sciences. Singapore: IACSIT Press, IPEDR, 17, pp. 77–85.

Applebee, A. (1977) Where Does Cinderella Live? In M. Meek, A. Warlow and G. Barton, *The Cool Web: The Pattern of Children's Reading*. London, Sydney, Toronto: The Bodley Head, pp. 51–58.

Arapera Royal Tangaere (1995) Personal communication. Conference Auckland, Early Childhood Education, New Zealand.

Armstrong, P. (2019) *Bloom's Taxonomy*. Vanderbilt University. Viewed 21 March 2019. http://cft.vanderbilt.edu.guides-sub-pages/blooms-taxonomy/.

Atkinson, P., Coffey, A., Delmont, S., Lofland, J. and Lofland, L. (eds) (2007) *Handbook of Ethnography*. London: Sage.

Athey, C. (1990) *Extending Thought in Young Children: A Parent-Teacher Partnership*. London: Paul Chapman.

Bacon, B. (1977) From Now to 1984. In M. Meek, G. Barton and A. Warlow (eds), *The Cool Web: The Pattern of Children's Reading*. London, Sydney, Toronto: The Bodley Head, pp. 129–133.

Bacon, K. (2012) 'Beings in Their Own Right'? Exploring Children and Young People's Sibling and Twin Relationships in the Minority World.' *Children's Geographies* 10 (3), pp. 307–319.

Bettelheim, B. (1976) *The Uses of Enchantment: The Meaning and Importance of Fairy Tales*. Great Britain: Thames and Hudson. (Currently published by Penguin).

Bettelheim, B. (1991) *The Uses of Enchantment: The Meaning and Importance of Fairy Tales*. Harmondsworth: Penguin.

Bilton, H. (1998) *Outdoor Play in the Early Years*. Oxon: David Fulton.

Blaise, M. and Brooker-Edwards, S. (eds) (2013) *The Sage Handbook of Play and Learning in Early Childhood*. London: Sage.

Bloom, B., Engelhart, M. and Furst, E. (1956) *The Taxonomy of Educational Objectives: Classification of Educational Goals Handbook 1*. New York: David McKay.

Booker, C. (2004) *The Seven Basic Plots*. New York: Continuum.

Bowlby, J. (2005) *The Making and Breaking of Affectional Bonds*. Oxon: Routledge.

Bredekamp, S. (2004) Play and School Readiness. In E. Zigler, D. Singer and S. Bishop-Josef (eds), *Children's Play: The Roots of Reading*. Washington, DC: Zero to Three, pp. 159–174.

Bredikyte, M. (2011) *The Zones of Proximal Development in Children's Play*. Oulu: University of Oulu.

Bredikyte, M. (ed) (2017) *Narrative Environments for Play and Learning (NEPL) Guidelines: For Kindergarten and School Teachers Working with 3–8 years-old-children*. ERASMUS: Lithuanian University of Educational Sciences.

Bredikyte, M. and Hakkarainen, P. (2017) Self Regulation in Children's Play. In T. Bruce, P. Hakkarainen and M. Bredikyte (eds), *The Routledge International Handbook of Early Childhood Play*. London: Routledge, pp. 246–259.

Brehony, K. (2001) *The Origins of Nursery Education Friedrich Froebel and the English System Froebel's Letters on the Kindergarten*. London, New York: Routledge.

Britton, J. (1970) *Language and Learning*. London: Allen Lane.

Britton, J. (1977) Response to Literature. In M. Meek, G. Barton and A. Warlow (eds), *The Cool Web; The Pattern of Children's Reading*. London, Sydney, Toronto: The Bodley Head, pp. 106–111.

Britton, J. (1988) The Role of Fantasy. In M. Meek, A. Warlow and G. Barton (eds), *The Cool Web: The Pattern of Children's Reading*. London: The Bodley Head, pp. 40–47.

Brooker, E., Blaise, M. and Edwards, S. (eds) (2014) *The Sage Handbook of Play and Learning in Early Childhood*. Boston: Sage, pp. 240–251.

Bruce, T. (1987) *Early Childhood Education*. London: Hodder and Stoughton.

Bruce, T. (1991) *Time to Play in Early Childhood Education*. London: Hodder and Stoughton.

Bruce, T. (1997) Adults and Children Developing Play Together. *European Early Childhood Education Research Journal* 5 (1), pp. 88–89.

Bruce, T. (2004) *Developing Learning in Early Childhood (Zero to Eight)*. London: Sage.

Bruce, T. (2005) *Early Childhood Education*. 3rd Edition. London: Hodder Education.

Bruce, T. (2015) *Early Childhood Education*. 5th Edition. London: Hodder Education.

Bruce, T. (2019) *Educating Young Children: A Lifetime Journey into a Froebelian Approach: The Selected Works of Tina Bruce*. Abingdon, New York: Routledge.

Bruce, T. (ed) (2010) *Early Childhood: A Student Guide*. 2nd Edition. London: Sage.

Bruce, T. (ed) (2012) *Early Childhood Practice: Froebel Today*. London: Sage.

Bruce, T. and Spratt, J. (2011) *Essentials of Literacy from 0–7: A Whole Child Approach to Communication, Language and Literacy.* 2nd Edition. London: Sage.

Bruce, T., Elfer, P. and Powell, S. (eds) with Werth, L. (2019) *The Routledge International Handbook of Froebel and Early Childhood Practice: Re-articulating Research and Policy.* Abingdon, New York: Routledge.

Bruce, T., Hakkarainen, P. and Bredikyte, M. (eds) (2018) *The Routledge International Handbook of Early Childhood Play.* London: Routledge.

Bruner, J. (1983) Play, Thought and Language. *Peabody Journal of Education, The Legacy of Nicholas Hobbs: Research on Education and Human Development in the Public Interest: Part 1 (Spring)* 60 (3), pp. 60–69.

Bruner, J. (1986) *Actual Minds, Possible Worlds.* Cambridge, MA: Harvard University Press.

Bruner, J. (1990) *Acts of Meaning.* Cambridge, MA: Harvard University Press.

Bruner, J., Wood, D. and Ross, G. (1976) The Role of Tutoring in Problem-solving. *Journal of Child Psychology and Psychiatry* 17, pp. 89–100.

Casey, T. and Robertson, J. (2016) *Loose Parts Play: A Toolkit.* Edinburgh: Inspiring Scotland in collaboration with Play Strategy Group and Scottish Government.

Christensen, P. and James, A. (2000) Introduction: Researching Children and Childhood: Cultures of Communication. In Christensen, P. and James, A. (eds), *Research with Children: Perspectives and Practices.* London: Routledge/Falmer, pp. 1–9.

Christensen, P. and James, A. (2001) What Are Schools For? The Temporal Experience of Children's Learning in Northern England. In L. Alanen and B. Mayall (eds), *Conceptualising Child–adult Relations.* London: Routledge/Falmer, pp. 70–85.

Clark, M. (ed) (2017) *Reading the Evidence: Synthetic Phonics and Literacy Learning.* Birmingham: Glendale Education.

CLPE (2019) Reflecting Realities: Survey of Ethnic Representation within UK Children's Literature 2018. London: Centre for Literacy in Primary Education.

CLPE (2019) *The Power of Pictures: Interim Report on Findings from the Research on the CLPE Power of Pictures Project.* London: Centre for Literacy in Primary Education.

Cole, M. (2015) Foreword. In G. Dowley McNamee (ed), *The High-Performing School: Story Acting in Head Start Classrooms.* Chicago, London: University of Chicago Press, pp. ix–xviii.

Consultative Committee on the Curriculum (CCC) and Committee On Primary Education (COPE) (1986) *Foundations of Writing: The Report of a Project on the Teaching of Writing at the Early Stages.* Edinburgh: Scottish Curriculum Development Service.

Corbett, P. (2008) *The National Strategies, Primary; Storytelling & Storymaking.* [Online] Available at: https://www.foundationyears.org.uk/files/2011/10/Story-Teling_Story-Making1.pdf [Accessed 22 April 2019].

Cozolino, L. (2006) *The Neuroscience of Human Relationships. Attachment and the Developing Social Brain.* New York: Norton.

Cremin, T., Flewitt, R., Mardell, B. and Swann, J. (eds) (2017) *Storytelling in Early Childhood Enriching Language, Literacy and Classroom Culture.* Abingdon: Routledge.

Cremin, T., Flewitt, R., Swann, J., Faulkner, D. and Kucirkova, N. (2018) Storytelling and Story-acting: Co-construction in Action. *Journal of Early Childhood Research* 16 (1), pp. 3–17.

Cremin, T., Swann, J., Flewitt, R., Falkner, D. and Kucirkova, N. (2013) *Evaluation Report of the MakeBelieve Arts Helicopter Technique of Storytelling and Story Acting.* London: Open University.

Daly, N., Limbrick, L. and Dix, P. (eds) (2018) *Children's Literature in a Multiliterate World.* London: UCL Institute of Education Press.

Department for Education and Skills (DfES) (2006) *Independent Review of the Teaching of Early Reading: Final Report, 'The Rose Review.'* London: DfES.

Donaldson, M. (1978) *Children's Minds.* London: Harper Perennial.

Dowley McNamee, G. (1915) *The High-Performing School: Story Acting in Head Start Classrooms.* Chicago, London: University of Chicago Press.

Dudley-Marling, C. and Lucas, K. (2009) Pathologizing the Language and Culture of Poor Children. *Language Arts* 86 (5), pp. 362–370.

Dunlop, A-W. (2018) The Child's Curriculum as a Gift. In C. Trevarthen, J. Delafield-Butt and A-W. Dunlop (eds), *A Child's Curriculum.* Oxford: Oxford University Press, pp. 212–234.

Dymock, S. (2007) Comprehension Strategy Instruction: Teaching Narrative Text Structure Awareness. *The Reading Teacher* 61, pp. 161–167.

Engel, S. (1995) *The Stories Children Tell: Making Sense of the Narratives of Childhood.* New York: W. H. Freeman.

Entwistle, J. (1970) *Child-centred Education.* London: Methuen.

Esteban-Guiart, M. and Moll, L. C. (2014) Funds of Identity: A New Concept Based on the Funds of Knowledge Approach. *Culture and Psychology* 20 (1), pp. 31–48.

Fabetti, R. (2005) Eyes and Silences. *Early Childhood Practice: The Journal for Multi-Professional Practice* 7 (1), pp. 8–12.

Fabian, H. and Dunlop, A. W. (2007) Outcomes of Good Practice in Transition Processes for Children Entering Primary School. *Working Paper 42.* The Hague, Netherlands: Bernard van Leer Foundation.

Feagans, L. and Appelbaum, M. I. (1986) Validation of Language Subtypes in Learning Disabled Children. *Journal of Educational Psychology* 78 (5), pp. 358–364.

Fernhold, A. (2014) *How Talking to Children Nurtures Language Development across SES and Culture.* [Lecture]Stanford: Stanford University.

Fiechtner, J. (2017) *Supporting Language Development.* Community Playthings. [Online] Available at: www.cabrillo.edu [Accessed 14 April 2017].

Freire, P. (1993) *Pedagogy of the Oppressed.* London: Penguin.

Froebel, F. (1826, Reprinted in 1967) In I. Lilley (ed), *Friedrich Froebel. A Selection from His Writings*. Cambridge, MA: Cambridge University Press.

Froebel, F. (1826) *The Education of Man*. New York: Appleton.

Froebel, F. (1852) Letter VI. In Brehony, K. (2001) *The Origins of Nursery Education: Frederich Froebel and the English System* Volume 2, *Froebel's Letters on the Kindergarten*. London, New York: Routledge.

Froebel, F. (1878) *Mother Play and Nursery Songs*. Translated by F. Dwight (songs) and J. Jarvis (prose). Boston: Lee and Shepherd.

Froebel, F. (1898) *The Education of Man*. Translated and annotated by W. N. Hailmann (2005). New York: Dover.

Froebel, F. (2004, Reprinted from the 1905 edition) *The Education of Man*. Honolulu: University Press of the Pacific.

Froebel, F. (c.1826, trans. 1885). *The Education of Man*. Translated by J. Jarvis. New York: A. Lovell.

Froebel. F. (1887) *The Education of Man*. New York: Appleton.

Frozen. (2013) (DVD) USA: Walt Disney Animation Studios.

Gent, M. and Heatley, M. (2009) *Little Book of Super Heroes*. Gravesend, UK: G2 Entertainment Limited.

Gibbons, P. (2002) *Scaffolding Language, Scaffolding Learning: Teaching Second Language Learners in the Mainstream Classroom*. Portsmouth, NH: Heinemann.

Gibbons, P. (2009) *English Learners, Academic Literacy and Thinking: Learning in the Challenge Zone*. Portsmouth, NH: Heinemann Educational Books.

Gill, S., Winters, D. and Friedman, D. (2006) Educators' Views of Pre-kindergarten and Kindergarten Readiness and Transition Practices. *Contemporary Issues in Early Childhood* 7 (3), pp. 213–227.

Gladstone, E. (2004) Leaparts Seminar. *Early Childhood Practice: The Journal for Multi-Professional Partnerships* 6 (2), pp. 97–98.

Goouch, K. and Lambirth, A. (2017) *Teaching Early Reading and Phonics: Creative Approaches to Early Literacy*. London: Sage.

Gopnik, A. Meltzoff, A. and Kuhl. P. (1999) *How Babies Think*. London: Nicolson and Weidenfeld.

Gottschall, J. (2012) *The Storytelling Animal: How Stories Make Us Human*. Boston: Houghton, Mifflin and Harcourt.

Gray, P. (2008) *The Value of Play 1: The Definition of Play Gives Insights*. [Online] Available at: https://www.psychologytoday.com/us/blog/freedom-learn/200811/the-value-play-i-the-definition-play-gives-insights [Accessed 18 April 2019].

Griffin, T., Hemphill, L., Camp, L. and Wolf, D. (2004) Oral Discourse in the Preschool Years and Later Literacy Skills. *First Language* 24, pp. 123–147.

Gura, P. (ed) (1992) *Exploring Learning: Young Children and Blockplay*. London: Paul Chapman.

Gussin-Paley, V. (1981) *Wally's Stories*. Cambridge, MA: Harvard University Press.

Gussin-Paley, V. (1984) *Boys and Girls: Superheroes in the Doll Corner*. Chicago: University of Chicago.

Gussin-Paley, V. (1986) *Mollie Is Three*. Chicago: University of Chicago Press.

Gussin-Paley, V. (1988) *Bad Boys Don't Have Birthdays*. Chicago: University of Chicago.

Gussin-Paley, V. (1990) *The Boy Who Would Be a Helicopter: The Uses of Storytelling in the Classroom*. Cambridge, MA: Harvard University Press.

Gussin-Paley, V. (2002) *The Boy Who Could Tell Stories*. [DVD] Muncie, IN: The Child Care Collection at Ball State University.

Gussin-Paley, V. (2004) *A Child's Work: The Importance of Fantasy Play*. Chicago: University of Chicago Press.

Gussin-Paley, V. (2010) *The Boy on the Beach*. Chicago: University of Chicago Press.

Hakkarainen, P. (2008) The Zone of Proximal Development in Play and Learning. *Cultural Historical Psychology* 4 (4), pp. 2–11.

Hakkarainen, P., Bredikyte, M., Jakkula, K. and Munter, H. (2013) Adult Play: Guidance and Children's Play Development in a Narrative Play World. *European Early Childhood Education Research Journal* 21 (2), pp. 213–225.

Hardy, B. (1977) Towards a Poetic Fiction: An Approach through Narrative. In M. Meek, A. Warlow and G. Barton (eds), *The Cool Web: The Pattern of Children's Reading*. London, Sydney, Toronto: The Bodley Head, pp. 12–23.

Hardy, L. (1912) *Diary of a Free Kindergarten*. London: Gay and Hancock.

Hardy, L. (1913) *The Diary of a Free Kindergarten*. Boston and New York: Houghton, Mifflin and Harcourt.

Hargreaves, A. and Dawe, R. (1990) Paths of Professional Development: Contrived Collegiality, Collaborative Culture, and the Case of Peer Coaching. *Teaching and Teacher Education* 6 (3), pp. 227–241.

Harrison, C. (1996) Family Literacy: Evaluation, Ownership and Ambiguity. *RSA Journal* 144 (5474), pp. 25–28.

Hart, B. and Risley, T. (1995) *Meaningful Differences in the Everyday Experience of Young American Children*. Baltimore: P. H. Brookes.

Hart, B. and Risley, T. R. (2003) The Early Catastrophe: The 30 Million Word Gap by Age 3. *American Educator* 27, pp. 4–9.

Haven, K. (2007) *Story Proof: The Science Behind the Startling Power of Story*. London: Libraries Unlimited.

Heathcote, D. (1999) *Drama as a Learning Medium*. London: Calender Island Publishers.

Hirsh-Pasek, K., Pace, A., Luo, R. and Michnick Golinkoff, R. (2017) Identifying Pathways between Socioeconomic Status and Language Development. *Annual Review of Linguistics* 3, pp. 285–308.

Holland, P. (2003) *We Don't Play with Guns Here: War, Weapon and Superhero Play in the Early Years*. Maidenhead: Open University Press.

Isaacs, S. (1930) *Intellectual Growth in Young Children*. London: Routledge.

Isaacs, S. (1968) *The Nursery Years*. London: Routledge.

James, A. (2002) Ethnography in the Study of Children and Childhood. In P. Atkinson, A. Coffey, S. Delamont, J. Lofland and L. Lofland (eds), *Handbook of Ethnography*. London: Sage, pp. 246–257.

James, A. and James, A. L. (2004) *Constructing Childhood*. New York: Palgrave and MacMillan.

James, A., Jenks, C. and Prout, A. (1998) *Theorizing Childhood*. Cambridge, MA: Polity.

Jenvey, V. and Newton, B. (2015) The Development of Theory of Mind and Its Role in Social Development in Early Childhood. In S. Robson and S. Flannery Quinn (eds), *The Routledge International Handbook of Young Children's Thinking and Understanding*. London: Routledge, pp. 163–178.

Johnston, R. and Watson, J. (2005) *The Effects of Synthetic Phonics Teaching on Reading and Spelling Attainment: A Seven Year Longitudinal Study*. Edinburgh: SEED.

Jones, G. (2002) *Killing Monsters: Why Children Need Fantasy, Super Heroes, and Make-Believe Violence*. New York: Basic Books.

Jung, C. (1995, Reprinted from the 1961 edition) *Memories, Dreams, Reflections*. London: Fontana.

Kalliala, M. (2006) *Play Culture in a Changing World*. Maidenhead: Open University Press.

Karpov, Y. (2005) *The Neo-Vygotskian Approach to Child Development*. Cambridge, MA: Cambridge University Press.

Kavanaugh, R. D. and Engel, S. (1998). The Development of Pretense and Narrative in Early Childhood. In N. Saracho and B. Spodek (eds), *Multiple Perspectives on Play in Early Childhood Education*. Albany State: State University of New York Press, pp. 80–89.

Kenner, C. (2000) *Home Pages: Literacy Links for Bilingual Children*. Stoke-on-Trent: Trentham Books.

Kermode, F. (1967) *The Sense of an Ending: Studies in the Theory of Fiction*. London: Open University Press.

Khimji, F. and Maunder, R. E. (2012) Mediational Tools in Story Construction: An Investigation of Cultural Influences on Children's Narratives. *Journal of Early Childhood Research* 10 (3), pp. 294–308.

Kruse Vaai, E. (2018) Within and Beyond the Blue Horizon: Creating Local and Global Identity through Reading: A Perspective from Samoa in the South Pacific. In N. Daly, L. Limbrick and P. Dix (eds), *Children's Literature in a Multiliterate World*. London: UCL Institute of Education Press, pp. 32–44.

Lahno, B. (2001) On the Emotional Character of Trust. *Ethical Theory and Moral Practice* 4 (2), pp. 171–189.

Landreth, G. (2002) *Play Therapy. The Art of the Relationship*. 2nd Edition. New York: Routledge.

Langer, S. (1944) *Philosophy in a New Key*. Boston: Harvard University Press.

Lee, T. (2016) *Princesses, Dragons and Helicopter Stories: Storytelling and Story Acting in the Early Years*. Abingdon: Routledge.

Lewis, C. S. (1969) On Stories. In M. Meek, A. Warlow and G. Barton (eds), *The Cool Web: The Pattern of Children's Reading.* London: The Bodley Head. pp. 76–90.

Lewis, G. (2003) *Teaching and Learning in a Circle: Dreaming of a New Reality.* The Third International Conference on Conferencing, Circles and other Restorative Practices, Minneapolis, Minnesota, pp. 8–10.

Lewis, M. (1999) Developing Children's Narrative Writing Using Story Structures. In: P. Goodwin (ed), *The Literate Classroom.* London: David Fulton, pp. 79–90.

Liebschner, J. (1992) *A Child's Work: Freedom and Guidance in Froebel's Educational Theory and Practice.* Cambridge, MA: Lutterworth.

Lilley, I. (1967) *Friedrich Froebel: A Selection of His Writings.* London: Cambridge University Press.

Lilley, I. (1967) *Friedrich Froebel: Cambridge Texts and Studies in the History of Education.* Cambridge, MA: Cambridge University Press.

Mackenzie, N. (2011) From Drawing to Writing: What Happens When You Shift Teaching Priorities in the First Six Months of School? *Australian Journal of Language & Literacy* 34 (3), pp. 322–340.

Majanovi-Umek, L., Fekonja-Peklaj, U. and Polesek, A. (2012) Parental Influence on the Development of Children's Storytelling. *European Early Childhood Education Research Journal* 20 (3), pp. 351–370.

Malloch, S. and Trevarthen, C. (eds) (2009) *Communicative Musicality: Exploring the Basis of Human Companionship.* Oxford: Oxford University Press.

Mandler, J. and Johnson, N. (1977) Remembrance of Things Parsed: The Story Structure and Recall. *Cognitive Psychology* 9, pp. 111–151.

McNair. L. (2016) *Rules, Rules, Rules, and We're Not Allowed to Skip: Exploratory Study: Listening to Children's Voices about the Transition to Primary One.* Unpublished Ph.D thesis. University of Edinburgh.

McNair, L. (2019) Case Study at Cowgate under 5's Centre. In T. Bruce, P. Elfer and S. Powell (eds), *The Routledge International Handbook of Froebel and Early Childhood Practice: Re-articulating Research and Policy.* London: Routledge, pp. 132–138.

McNamee, G., McLane, J., Cooper, P. and Kerwin, S. (1985) Cognition and Affect in Early Literacy Development. *Early Child Development and Care* 20 (4), pp. 229–244.

Meek, M. (1985) Play and Paradoxes: Some Considerations for Imagination and Language. In G. Wells and J. Nicolls (eds), *Language and Learning: An Interactional Perspective.* London: Falmer Press, pp. 41–58.

Meek, M. (1996) *Information and Book Learning.* Stroud: Thimble Press.

Meek, M., Warlow, A. and Barton, G. (1977) *The Cool Web: The Pattern of Children's Reading.* London: The Bodley Head.

Mellgreen, E. and Gustafsson, K. (2011) Early Childhood Literacy and Children's Multimodal Expressions in Preschool. In N. Pramling and

I. Pramling Samuelsson (eds), *Educational Encounters: Nordic Studies in Early Childhood Didactics. International Perspectives on Early Childhood Education and Development* 4. Dordrecht: Springer, pp. 173–190.

Michaelis, E. and Moore, H. (1891) *Froebel's Letters on the Kindergarten trans. from Kindergarten-Briefe (1887)*. London: s.n.

Mills, G. (1976) *Hamlet's Castle: The Study of Literature as a Social Experience*. Austin, TX: University of Texas Press.

Moska, M. (2010) I Want to Play When I Go to School: Children's Views on the Transition to School from Kindergarten. *Australasian Journal of Early Childhood* 35 (3), pp. 134–139.

Moss, E. (1977) The Peppermint Lesson. In M. Meek, A. Warlow and G. Barton, *The Cool Web: The Pattern of Children's Reading*. London, Sydney, Toronto: The Bodley Head, pp. 140–142.

Moss, P. (2014) *Transformative Change and Real Utopias in Early Childhood Education – A Story of Democracy, Experimentation and Potentiality*. Oxon: Routledge.

Nelson, K. and Seidman, S. (1984) Playing with Scripts. In I. Bretherton (ed), *Symbolic Play*. New York: Academic Press, pp. 45–72.

Nicolopoulou, A. (1996) Narrative Development in Social Context. In D. Slobin, J. Gerhardt, J. Guo and A. Kyrotzis (eds), *Social Interaction, Social Context and Language Essays in Honour of Susan Erin-Tripp*. Hillsdale, NJ: Erlbaum Associates, pp. 369–390.

Nicolopolou, A. (2007) The Interplay of Play and Narrative in Children's Development: Theoretical Reflections and Concrete Examples. In A. Goncu and S. Gaskins (eds), *Play and Development: Evolutionary, Sociocultural, and Functional Perspectives*. Abingdon: Taylor Francis Group, pp. 247–273.

Nicolopulou, A. (2016) Promoting Oral Narrative Skills through a Peer-oriented Storytelling and Story-acting Practice. In T. Cremin, R. Flewitt, B. Mardell and J. Swann (eds), *Storytelling in Early Childhood: Enriching Language, Literacy and Classroom Culture*. London: Routledge.

Nicolopoulou, A. (2016) Young Children's Pretend Play and Storytelling as Modes of Narrative Activity: From Complementarity to Cross-Fertilization? In L. Stirling and S. Douglas (eds), *Children's Play, Pretense, and Story: Studies in Culture, Context and Autism Spectrum Disorder*. New York: Routledge, pp. 7–28.

Nicolopoulou, A., Barbosa de Sa, A., Ilgaz, H. and Brockmeyer, C. (2010) Using the Transformative Power of Play to Educate Hearts and Minds: From Vygotsky to Vivian Paley and Beyond. *Mind, Culture and Activity* 17, pp. 42–58.

Nicolopoulou, A., McDowell, J. and Brockmeyer, C. (2006) Narrative Play and Emergent Literacy: Storytelling and Story Acting Meet Journal Writing. In D. Singer, R. Golinkoff and K. Hirsh-Pasek (eds), *Play = Learning: How Play Motivates and Enhances Children's Cognitive and Social-Emotional Growth*. Oxford: Oxford University Press, pp. 124–144.

Nicolopoulou, A., Richner, E. (2007) From Actors to Agents to Person: The Development of Character Representation in Young Children's Narratives. *Child Development* 78 (2), 412–429.

Okri, B. (2015) *The Mystery Feast. Thoughts on Storytelling.* West Hoathly: Clairview Books.

Organisation for Economic Co-operation and Development (2002) *Reading for Change: Performance and Engagement across Countries. Results from PISA 2000.* OECD.

Palacios, A. (2017) To Reach a Place of Safety, Article with Photos, *New Internationalist*, July/August, pp. 34–35.

Pascal, C., Bertram, T. and Rouse, L. (2019) *Getting It Right in the Early Years Foundation Stage: A Review of the Evidence.* Centre for Research in Early Childhood.

Pellegrini, A. and Galda, L. (1993) Ten Years After: A Reexamination of Symbolic Play and Literacy Research. *Reading Research Quarterly*, 28 (2), pp. 162–175.

Poesche, H. (1890) Propagation and Extension. In K. Brehony (ed, 2001), *The Origins of Nursery Education Friedrich Froebel and the English System: Froebel's Letters on the Kindergarten.* London, New York: Routledge, pp. 175–281.

Popova, M. (2014) *Einstein on Fairy Tales and Education.* Brain Pickings. [Online] Available at: https://www.brainpickings.org/2014/03/14/einstein-fairy-tales/. [Accessed 23 February 2019].

Popper, S. (2013) *Rethinking Superhero and Weapon Play.* Maidenhead: Open University Press.

Puroila, A-M., Estola, E. and Syrjala, L. (2012) Does Santa Exist? Children's Everyday Narratives as Dynamic Meeting Places in a Day Care Context. *Early Child Development and Care* 182 (2), pp. 191–206.

Rathnarsdottir, H. (2006) Constructing the Tools for Participation in Culture and Democracy: Children's Language Proficiency at Age 5-6 Years and the Implications of Individual Variation. EECERA Conference keynote, Reykjavik, 1 September 2006.

Riley, J. and Reedy, D. (2000) *Developing Writing for Different Purposes.* London: Paul Chapman.

Roberts, R. (2010) *Wellbeing from Birth.* London: Sage.

Rogoff, B. (1993) Commentary. *Human Development* 36, pp. 24–26.

Rogoff. B. (2003) *The Cultural Nature of Human Development.* Oxford: Oxford University Press.

Ronnberg, A. and Martin, K. (eds) (2010) *The Book of Symbols. Reflections on Archetypal Images.* Archive for Research in Archetypal Symbolism, Köln: Taschen.

Rosen, M. (2015) *A Great Big Cuddle: Poems for the Very Young.* London: Walker Books.

Rubin, Z. (1983) The Skills of Friendship. In M. Donaldson, R. Grieve and C. Pratt (eds), *Early Childhood Development and Education: Readings in Psychology*. Oxford: Basil Blackwell, pp. 25–33.

Rumelhart, D. (1975) Notes on a Schema for Stories. In D. Bobrow and A. Collins (eds), *Representation and Understanding: Studies in Cognitive Science*. New York: Academic, pp. 211–236.

Saifer, S. (2010) Higher Order Play and Its Role in Development and Education. *Psychological Science and Education* 3, pp. 38–50.

Salmon, K., Evans, I. M., Moskowitz, S., Grouden, M., Parkes, F. and Miller, E. (2012) The Components of Young Children's Emotion Knowledge: Which Are Enhanced by Adult Emotion Talk? *Social Development* 22 (1), pp. 94–110.

Sands, L., Carr, M. and Lee, W. (2012) Question-asking and Question-exploring. *European Education Research Journal* 20 (4), pp. 553–564. http://dx.doi.org /10.1080/1350293X.2012.737705.

Schultz, K. (2015) Listening in Pedagogy of Trust. In L. Waks (ed), *Listening to Teach – Beyond Didactic Pedagogy*. Albany: State University of New York Press, pp. 149–166.

Scottish Government (2013) *Play Strategy for Scotland: Our Vision*. The Scottish Government. [Online] Available at: https://www.gov.scot/publications/ play-strategy-scotland-vision/. [Accessed 23 March 2019].

Scottish Government (2014) *Building the Ambition*. Edinburgh: Scottish Government.

Shannon, P. (2000) A Marxist reading of reading education. *Cultural Logic*, 4 (1), pp.1–13.

Shapiro, L. and Hudson, J. (1991) Tell Me a Make-believe Story: Coherence and Cohesion in Young Children's Picture-elicited Narratives. *Developmental Psychology* 12, pp. 960–974.

Slade, A. and Wolf, D. (1994) *Children at Play*. Oxford: Oxford University Press.

Smilansky, S. (1968) *The Effects of Sociodramatic Play on Disadvantaged Children*. New York: Wiley.

Stanzel, F. K. (1984) *A Theory of Narrative*. Cambridge, MA: Cambridge University Press.

Stein, N. and Glenn, C. (1979) An Analysis of Story Comprehension in Elementary School Children. In R. Freedle (ed), *New Directions in Discourse Processing*. Norwood, NJ: Ablex, pp. 53–120.

Storr, C. (1977) Things That Go Bump in the Night. In M. Meek, A. Warlow and G. Barton, *The Cool Web: The Pattern of Children's Reading*. London, Sydney, Toronto: The Bodley Head, pp. 120–128.

Sutton-Smith, B. (1997) *The Ambiguity of Play*. Cambridge, MA, London: Harvard University Press.

Swanson, A. M. M. (1975) *The History of Edinburgh's Early Nursery Schools*. Edinburgh: Howie and Seath.

Taylor, D. (1983) *Family Literacy*. London: Heinemann.

Thomas, L. Jack, J. and Crowley, J. (2017) Family?...Not Just Blood. Discursive Constructions of "Family" in Adult Former Foster Children's Narratives. *Journal of Communication* 17 (2) pp. 253–328.

Tisdall, K., Davis, J. and Gallagher, M. (2009) *Researching with Children and Young People – Research Design, Methods and Analysis*. London: Sage.

Tolkien, J. (1964) *Tree and Leaf*. London: Allen and Unwin.

Torgerson, C., Brooks, G., Gascoine, L. and Higgins, S. (2018) Phonics: Reading Policy and the Evidence of Effectiveness from a Systematic 'Tertiary' Review. *Research Papers in Education* 34 (2), pp. 208–238.

Tovey, H. (2013) *Bringing the Froebel Approach to Your Early Years Practice*. Abingdon: Routledge.

Trevarthen, C. (1993) Playing into Reality: Conversations with the Infant Communicator. *Winnicott Stories* 7, pp. 67–84.

Trevarthen, C. (1998) The Child's Need to Learn a Culture. In M. Woodhead, D. Faulkner and K. Littleton (eds), *Cultural Worlds of Early Childhood*. London: Routledge in Association with Open University Press, pp. 87–100.

Trevarthen, C. (2002) *Learning in Companionship*. Edinburgh: University of Edinburgh and University of Strathclyde.

Trevarthan, C. (2004) Learning about Ourselves from Children: Why a Growing Human Brain Needs Interesting Companions. *Annual Report: Hokkaido University Research and Clinical Centre for Child Development* 26, pp. 9–44.

Vygotsky, L. (1967) Play and Its Role in the Mental Development of the Child. *Soviet Psychology* 5, pp. 6–18.

Vygotsky, L. (1976) Play and Its Role in the Mental Development of the Child. In J. Bruner, A. Jolly and K. Sylva (eds), *Play: Its Role in Development and Evolution*. New York: Basic Books.

Vygotsky, L. (1978) *Mind in Society: The Development of Higher Psychological Processes*. Cambridge, MA: Harvard University Press.

Walter, C. and Briggs, J. (2012) *What Professional Development Makes the Most Difference to Teachers?* Oxford: Oxford University Press.

Wellman, R., Lewis, B., Freebairn, L., Avrich, A., Hansen, A. and Stein, C. (2011) Narrative Ability of Children with Speech Sound Disorders and the Prediction of Later Literacy Skills. *Language, Speech and Hearing Services in Schools* 42, pp. 561–579.

Whinnett, J. (2012) Gifts and Occupations. In T. Bruce (ed), *Early Childhood Practice: Froebel Today*. London: Sage, pp. 121–136.

Whitebread, D. and Jameson, H. (2010) Play beyond the Foundation Stage: Storytelling, Creative Writing and Self-regulation in Able 6–7 Year Olds. In J. Moyles (ed), *The Excellence of Play*. 3rd Edition. Maidenhead: Open University Press, pp. 95–107.

Whitehead, M. (2000, February 2) *Keep in Touch – Communication Forms*. Nursery World. Retrieved from: www.nurseryworld.co.uk/nursery-world/news/1081474/touch-communication-forms

Whitehead, M. (2007) *Developing Language and Literacy with Young Children.* 3rd Edition. London: Sage.

Whitehead, M. (2004) *Language and Literacy in the Early Years 0–7.* 2nd Edition. London: Sage.

Whitehead, M. (2010) *Language and Literacy in the Early Years 0–7.* 4th Edition London: Sage.

Winnicott, D. (1971) *Playing and Reality.* Hammondsworth: Penguin.

Wong Powell, J. (2016) Redefining the Teacher's Role in Children's Play. *Selected Papers of the Association for Teacher Education in Europe, Spring Conference 2015.* Newcastle Upon Tyne: Cambridge Scholars Publishing.

Wright, C., Diener, M. L. and Kemp, J. L. (2013) Storytelling Dramas as Community Building Activity in an Early Childhood Classroom. *Early Childhood Education Journal* 41 (3), pp. 197–210.

Index